CREATING WINNING CAREER SYSTEMS

Unique Insights for Underdogs & Undervalued Workers Who Want a Rewarding Career While Improving the World

By

Coach Teddy Edouard

Coaching for Better Learning

This book is designed to offer guidance on career and professional development. But its teaching should not be taken as legal advice and services. If you need legal help, consult a licensed legal professional.

While Coaching for Better Learning LLC has made every effort to provide accurate information at the time of publication, neither the publisher nor the author assumes any responsibility for errors and changes that happen after the release of this book. The author and the publisher have no control over and do not assume any responsibility and liability for third-party websites and their content.

Copyright © 2020 by Coaching For Better Learning, LLC

Copyright © 2020 Teddy Edouard

All rights reserved.

ISBN: 979-8-6539-8198-2

Dedication

The Coaching for Better Learning team and I dedicate this book to all the underdogs and undervalued employees that make the world go around, especially those impacted by the economic crisis caused by COVID-19.

Contents

Dedication iii
Contents iv
Foreword x
    You are not alone x
    Good news x
Introduction xii
    Napoleon Bonaparte's worst nightmare xii
    The Philly underdogs xiii
    The underdog the tennis world never saw coming xiv
    You can, too. xv
    But this book might not be for you. xv
    Our focal point xvi
    What's on the pages xvi
    Before going further, ask yourself this: xvii
CHAPTER 1 1
A Less Obvious Choice 1
    A typical average employee 2
    A warning for professionals 3
    The man who refused to maintain the status quo 4
    What can underdogs and undervalued employees do? 5
    The price 6
    The benefits 7
    Reflection questions 8
CHAPTER 2 9

Your Work vs. Your Job 9
    The difference… 10
    What accepting a job means 10
    A deadly career trap 11
    What can underdogs and undervalued employees do? .. 12
    Bettering your luck 12
    What a job brings 13
    Reflection questions 14
CHAPTER 3 15
A Highly Neglected Career Success Factor 15
    The design whisperer 15
    Hiring mistakes 16
    What most employees get wrong 17
    What can underdogs and undervalued employees do? .. 17
    The key to becoming valuable 18
    What does energy have to do with it? 19
    How energy management affects performance 20
    You waste your energy, you lose. 21
    Reflection questions 21
CHAPTER 4 23
Most Employee Training Sessions Aren't for Employees 23
    Traditional training 23
    Scary training and learning stories 25
    A distorted view of training and learning 26
    The hidden purpose of most employee training… 26
    What can underdogs and undervalued employees do? .. 27
    Take the wheel. 27

Reflection questions 28

CHAPTER 5 29
The Quintessential Move for Career Success 29
- What outliers do 30
- What can underdogs and undervalued employees do? .. 31
- What your system should include 32
- Getting your own guide 33
- Reflection questions 34

CHAPTER 6 35
A Talent Differentiator 35
- Simone Biles 35
- TD Jakes 35
- Marie Callender 36
- Chris Garner 36
- What mastery means 37
- What can underdogs and undervalued employees do? .. 38
- The road to mastery 39
- Concrete actions 40
- Reflection questions 41

CHAPTER 7 42
A Common Career Misconception 42
- So, is work experience valuable? 43
- Don't let years of work experience fool you. 43
- A blessing and a curse 44
- What can underdogs and undervalued employees do? .. 45
- Reflection questions 47

CHAPTER 8 48

The Art of Contribution 48
    See, think, do 48
    Senator Obama in Illinois 49
    What can underdogs and undervalued employees do? .. 50
    What contributions look like… 51
    Where to start… 51
    Reflection questions 52
CHAPTER 9 54
Opportunity in the Noise 54
    See, think, do 54
    An ocean of information and data 54
    Problem and opportunity 55
    Forty Second Boyd 56
    Chieko Asakawa 56
    Travis Kalanick and Garrett Camp 57
    Brian Chesky, Joe Gebbia and Nathan Blecharczyk 57
    George Washington Carver 57
    The PayPal mafia 57
    Seth Godin 57
    Victor B. Lawrence 58
    Good seeing skills 58
    What can underdogs and undervalued employees do? .. 59
    What it takes to develop excellent seeing skills 59
    Taking action 60
    Reflection questions 61
CHAPTER 10 62
Leading Instead of Hiding 62

See, think, do. 62
Examples of execution 63
What can underdogs and undervalued employees do? .. 64
What the art of execution looks like in a workday 64
Stop at nothing 65
Below are examples of things you can execute: 66
Reflection questions 66

CHAPTER 11 68
Invisible Career Traps and Killers 68
The roadblock 68
Kawhi Leonard 69
What can underdogs and undervalued employees do? .. 70
Helpful connections 71
What cultivating a positive attitude means 72
Workplace foolishness 72
Reflection questions 73

CHAPTER 12 74
Creating the Future 74
Drones in the job market 75
Elon Musk's prediction 75
Education left the classroom 76
Robots in the marketplace 76
Post-COVID-19 observations 77
What can underdogs and undervalued employees do after COVID-19? 78
Where to start… 79
Reflection questions 81

CONCLUSION 82

Now what? 82
Further Reading 84
Interesting and Relevant podcasts 86
Acknowledgment 87
References 88
Index 93
About the Author 96
About Coaching for Better Learning LLC 97

Foreword

Maybe all you want, like many professionals, is to get jobs you like, build a rewarding career and make a difference in the world. You also want to feel valued and respected. So, you labor away and think you are doing your best, yet you can't get any traction.

You, therefore, feel stuck in non-rewarding, dead-end jobs, frustrated about your lack of career growth. In other words, you find yourself in an underdog or undervalued position despite your excellent work ethic and competence. I feel you because I have been there, too.

You are not alone

Look at the research. According to Gallup, more than 40% of U.S. employees feel underpaid, less than 35% feel their work is engaging and only about 27% strongly believe in their company's values.

But there's more. *Workplace Insights* reported that more than 33% of U.S. workers feel undervalued by their supervisors and more than 33% feel dissatisfied with their jobs.

According to the Center for Workplace Mental Health, high workplace stress causes 120,000 deaths annually in the U.S. and leads to a $190 billion loss in health care costs per year. And things might get even worse or more challenging in the post-COVID-19 world.

Let me stop here before I drive you into depression.

Good news

You might not have enough resources and connections to compete and get ahead in your professional career. But this should not stop you in your tracks.

As Elon Musk, founder of Tesla and SpaceX, recommends, if your competitors have more assets or resources than you do, you should leverage innovation. Jumping on the career innovation train is one of the best ways to escape harsh career competition. But how do you climb aboard?

The key to lasting and innovative career improvement, growth and success is to use *systems*. Thus, this book aims to show undervalued professionals how to use unconventional moves—systematic moves—to develop satisfying careers while making a difference in the world.

Why systems? Because they are powerful. Let me give you an example. Brothers Maurice and Richard McDonald, the owners of the first McDonald's, didn't invent hamburgers or French fries. They just developed a system to cook and deliver hamburgers and French fries in minutes at a low cost. That's what ended up making their restaurant so valuable. It was by using a *system* that they were able to reach their *goal* of becoming successful entrepreneurs.

I encourage you to approach these pages with an open mind since some of the career moves differ from traditional career guidance. Read and keep the ideas you want or need and feel free to disagree with and ignore the rest.

This book project started more than a year before the COVID-19 health and economic crisis hit the world. But I've adjusted the content to address issues workers will face in the post-COVID-19 world and workplace. You'll find it in Chapter 12. But before you start reading, here are three questions to ponder:

- What is holding my career back?
- How am I making an impact?
- What am I known for at work?

Having the answers to these three questions in the back of your mind as you read will help you decide which information in this book is most valuable to you.

Now enjoy your reading process!

Introduction

Let's start with the story of one of the most fascinating underdogs or undervalued employees who has ever walked the earth.

Nikola Tesla, the well-known electrical engineer who invented alternative current (AC), was an underdog when he worked for the famous American inventor and businessman, Thomas Edison. He left after six months on the job and until now, it's been hard to know exactly why he left. But what happened in the electrical energy market after Tesla left made the reason more than obvious.

Tesla created AC as an alternative to Edison's direct current (DC). Tesla and his work got noticed by businesspeople and the press since he no longer operated under the shadow of the great Thomas Edison. He, therefore, gained influence and recognition for his genius.

Edison tried to stop Tesla but in vain. The electrical energy market had already made room for Tesla's brilliance, hard work and innovation. It's pretty hard to put the good-idea genie back in the bottle once it's out.

Tesla left because he felt stuck in a dead-end job. He took charge of his career and, as a result, became an inventor the world would be talking about for years to come. And his remarkable work makes the world a better place.

Napoleon Bonaparte's worst nightmare

Have you ever heard of Toussaint Louverture? He was a Haitian slave who didn't even know his date of birth. He was known to be small and weak. But even as an underdog, he managed to study and learn military and political strategies from his oppressors: the French and the Spanish.

Toussaint transformed his life into that of a world-class revolutionary. How? He manipulated the French, Spanish and

British into submission. He led the first slave rebellion in the new world. He defeated the French army—Napoleon Bonaparte's army! —to establish the first autonomous black territory in the Caribbean in 1801.

However, Toussaint was kidnapped, brutalized and imprisoned in La Bastille in France until his death. After his death, it was too late for France to stop the revolutionary wind in Saint Domingue. Why? The freedom train had already left the station. The smell of freedom had already spread all over Saint Domingue. Consequently, Haiti declared her independence as the first, free black nation in the Americas in 1804.

Many admire Toussaint for his brilliance. The man moved from being a slave and a nobody to finding a silver lining and becoming a symbol of freedom, resilience and hope in a world living under the reign of slavery.

The Philly underdogs

Now let's take a look at a great American football underdog story. It's about Nicholas Edward Foles—also known as Saint Nick to Philadelphia Eagles fans. In 2017, Nick was a backup quarterback for the Eagles, sitting on the bench watching his team play football. You might think this was a great job. No, it wasn't.

Being a backup quarterback technically means Nick was not good enough to be the starter—let alone the leader—of the team. But in week 14 of the 2017 football season, the worst and best things happened to the Eagles at the same time. Let me tell you more…

The worst thing: the Eagles' starting quarterback got injured and was out for the rest of the season. A cloud of doubt, panic and hopelessness hovered over the team. It was like seeing the captain of a cruise ship become terribly seasick in the middle of the deep, blue sea only halfway to the destination. Or like in a disaster movie when the pilot dies in the middle of the flight.

The best thing: The Eagles got to rely on an underdog quarterback who was just waiting for an opportunity, a crack in the wall, to show the world what he had to offer.

Long story short, when Nick started in week 15, people doubted him, counted him out and did not believe he had what it took. Of course, he made mistakes, but he learned and adjusted as fast he could. Consequently, he accomplished a masterstroke no one saw coming— one that Philadelphians will remember for decades to come.

Nick led the Eagles to its third Super Bowl game and defeated the New England Patriots by outplaying the best quarterback and best coach of all time, Tom Brady and Bill Belichick, to give the City of Brotherly Love its first Superbowl trophy in franchise history. As if this were not enough, Nick was named the Most Valuable Player of Super Bowl LII.

The underdog the tennis world never saw coming

The now-famous tennis player, Naomi Osaka, also offers a classic underdog story in the sport of tennis. She put herself in the land of legends without asking permission.

For several years, Naomi was an unknown tennis player, but she was determined to establish herself and make a name in the tennis world. She was ranked the 406th female tennis player in the world when she was 16 years old. Guess what? As I write this, she is 22 years old and #1 in the world.

What? How did she jump to #1 so fast?

She is a hardworking, determined and consistent player who stops at nothing on the way to accomplishing her dreams. For example, it has been reported that she gave up her U.S. citizenship so she could play for Japan on the world stage. In other words, she saw a crack in the wall and went right through it.

As a result of her hard work, persistence and strategic moves, she did the unthinkable: she embodied *veni, vidi, vici*. She came, saw and conquered the tennis world. "How so?" you may ask. She defeated the world's best players one after another to reach the U.S. Open (the final tennis competition of the year) in 2018. Then she took down the queen of tennis, the G.O.A.T. (Greatest Of All Time), Serena Williams. Consequently, Naomi moved from being an underdog to becoming the first Japanese and Asian player to ever win a Grand Slam (the four most important tennis championships in the world) and, above all, she became the #1-woman tennis player in the globe.

You can, too.

Although Tesla, Toussaint, Nick and Naomi have different life stories, deep down they have several things in common. They started as underdogs and undervalued talents but took control to become forces to be reckoned with.

But how did they reach the pinnacle, the zenith, the peak of the mountain? What did they do? Like other successful underdogs, they undoubtedly had a playbook or a system and used the right moves at the right time.

> The good news is you, too, can change your story, control your career and become the professional you dream to be—if you understand how to build winning systems and have the guts to do what it takes. This book will share ideas to help you do that.

But this book might not be for you.

If you enjoy pity parties, passing the blame or being just an OK professional, this book won't work for you. If you are also looking for motivational punchlines, these pages won't help either. It's also not a book on job searching, job applications and interviewing techniques and strategies.

However:

- If you are living under a cloud of humiliation from being disrespected, undervalued and passed over for promotions you deserve, this is your book.

- If you are treated as an average commodity who is disposable and you want to change that, these chapters are for you.
- If you struggle to navigate the workplace, maintain good relationships and excel in what you do, these pages are for you.
- If you want to serve, lead, and make the world a better place for other people, I wrote these ideas especially for you.

Simply put, this book is for underdogs in need of opportunities to show the world the giants, the mavericks and the trailblazers they really are.

In other words, the coaching insights shared in this book are for folks who want to raise their professional standing, break away from the crowd, and add a new, *better* chapter to their own underdog story. If this sounds like you, keep reading.

Our focal point

When reading about or watching underdog stories, most people focus on where the main protagonists started (underdog status) and on their achievements (linchpins, champions), but miss the view of what happened behind the scenes: *the system and the process.*

This book, for the most part, will reveal secrets, debunk myths and focus on *processes and systems*—the behind-the-scenes stuff that leads to effectiveness, sound decisions and career progress. It shares advice on unescapable professional issues. In so doing, it challenges belief systems: the way one views work, responsibility and change.

What's on the pages

While this book presents a roadmap—a system—that includes action steps to help professionals escape harsh competition, it does not promise magical transformation and solutions.

- Chapter 1 describes a foundational career principle that should not be ignored.
- Chapter 2 clarifies a common misunderstanding that derails professional careers.
- Chapter 3 describes a common mistake related to employees' value.
- Chapter 4 explains why most employee training initiatives are not what we think they are.
- Chapter 5 contrasts career goals to personal development systems and provides critical recommendations.
- Chapters 6 and 7 address mastery and debunk the oldest myth in the job market.
- Chapters 8 and 9 explore two major success factors no serious professional can afford to overlook.
- Chapter 10 describes the art of execution.
- Chapters 11 and 12 discuss indispensable skills, especially for a post-COVID-19 world. These skills determine how far underdogs can get in their professional careers.

Now, it's time for us to start our journey to a better us and see what we are made of. See you in Chapter 1, or in whichever chapter your curious mind takes you to first.

Before going further, ask yourself this:

- Is this book relevant to my career needs?
- Should I read the entire book, or should I pick the chapters relevant to my needs?
- How can I approach reading this book in a systematic way?

CHAPTER 1

A Less Obvious Choice

What kind of professional do you want to be? Being like everybody else or doing what others do doesn't sound like a promising choice. As the famous American writer and speaker, Seth Godin, said, "In a crowded marketplace, fitting in is failing. In a busy marketplace, not standing out is the same as being invisible."

Let's reflect on five questions:

- Can you afford to be an average professional?
- Will you be satisfied with living on everybody's agenda but your own?
- How satisfied are you with letting other people dictate your career choice and decisions?
- Are you happy to work dead-end, boring and emotionally draining jobs?
- Are you OK with an average career? (Some people are.)

Let's take a look at the summary for job cuts (layoffs or terminations) on tradingeconomy.com. Here are the job-cut figures for October 2019:

> U.S.-based employers announced plans to cut 50, 275 jobs from their payrolls in October 2019....The technology sector led all sectors with 15, 898 announced cuts, bringing the year-to-date total to 56,155, the third-highest total for any industry through October. Health care companies

announced 5,400 cuts while retail announced 6,127. So far this year, employers have announced plans to cut 515,441 jobs from their payrolls, 16.6 percent higher than the same period last year. It is the highest January-October total since 2015.

These jobs-cut numbers came to about six million jobs. However, compared to jobs lost in March 2020 due to COVID-19, this is a drop in a bucket.

Let's be straightforward here. Job cuts mean that real people with bills to pay lose their jobs. But the job market could not care less. Yes, the job market is cruel, merciless and ruthless. And it's not going to change anytime soon.

Even during stable economic times, when push comes to shove and companies want to balance their budget, which type of employees do they sacrifice, abandon or eliminate first and fastest? The staff that is easy to replace in no time.

And after a mass layoff due to an economic crisis, when employers resume normal operations, guess which type of workers they want back as soon as possible. The high performers, of course. You get the point.

A typical average employee

See, average employees are easy to spot because they all have certain traits. They…

- go by the book, follow orders and do only what they are told.
- focus on basic expectations and job descriptions and perform within the limits.
- meet the acceptable job performance so they don't get fired and repeat this cycle over and over again for 25 or 30 years.
- believe in "what you paid for is what you get."

- are quick to blame everyone and everything else for their shortcomings, except themselves.
- go with the flow, fit in, do what most employees do and complete average tasks instead of doing work worth talking about.
- build a career for their benefit only.

Thus, average employees are easy targets. Any wind of economic instability, restructuring or merger can blow their jobs away.

> The worst thing that can happen to a professional is to become an experienced, hardworking and *average* employee doing average work that meets minimum standards. Why? Because it leads to a false sense of expertise and stability.

What's worse, this type of employee is prone to turn into a company's worst nightmare by becoming a staff that fights change, innovation and new ideas from all angles.

A warning for professionals

If your company's employee evaluation or performance appraisal template is all that is needed to reflect your work, you are in trouble. Why?

The template was designed with the average worker in mind, not for the linchpin. So, meeting minimal standards is like committing career suicide. It's a way to ask employers to treat you as disposable. Maybe you are thinking, "But I don't get paid enough to do more than what's required."

See, when you perform average work, based on how you are treated or paid, you suck the lifeblood out of your career and personal brand. It's like shooting yourself in the foot and hoping to outperform your competitors.

> The truth is, when it comes to standing out on the job, the saying "you get what you pay for" *is not applicable*. That kind of thinking is a trap that leads to career stagnation and destruction.

As a side note, you don't get to perform average work and toot your own horn, expecting the job market to treat you as special. What your work says about you is way more valuable than whatever you tell people about your work.

The man who refused to maintain the status quo

Take Lee Iacocca's story. He started in the engineering department of Ford Motor Company, but requested a transfer to sales and became assistant sales manager in the Philadelphia District.

In 1956, sales of Ford's automobiles hit rock bottom in Lee's district. In fact, the district was ranked last in sales nationwide. Lee analyzed the struggle, the crisis and the threat, and turned the ordeal into an opportunity. What he did next changed his career and his life forever.

Lee created a bold marketing plan: the "56 for '56" marketing program. The "56 for '56" slogan meant with a 20% down payment, a customer could buy a 1956 Ford by paying $56 a month for three years. His plan turned the Philadelphia district into the #1 district in the nation in units sold.

"Did Lee get promoted?" you may ask. Not only did he get promoted, but Lee quickly rose to become president of Ford Motor Company.

Ralph Kisiel of the *Automotive News* reported:

> Iacocca's '56 for '56' idea won him a promotion to district manager of Washington, D.C. Just four years later, in November 1960, Iacocca was

elected a vice president and was appointed general manager of Ford Division.

Remember Lee Iacocca's original title? Yes, it was "assistant sales manager." Now, ask yourself, where was the sales manager? And what were the other sales managers across the nation doing? They probably got stuck doing work that met basic standards and maintained the status quo.

One more thing. Lee Iacocca did not major in marketing. This leads us to the main point of this chapter:

What can underdogs and undervalued employees do?

Career Move #1 – Work with a sense of purpose.

Working with a sense of purpose means building a professional career bigger than ourselves for the benefit of humankind. It signifies doing quality work on any job in an effort to serve and help others in a way that goes beyond employers' expectations.

> Folks who work with a sense of purpose offer unforgettable customer experience, build genuine connections and make life easier. They are not out to cheat the system and call it a day. Instead, they are personally invested in building people up and making a real difference.

Those who work with purpose don't rely on their employer's motivational incentives and gimmicks to perform at their best. That's because their inspiration comes from their commitment to serve—and to make the world a better place.

Seth Godin calls this kind of commitment "remarkable work." The media executive and philanthropist, Oprah Winfrey, describes it as the way you "touch people's lives." Pastor and author, Myles Munroe, calls it "your own work." Author and speaker, Simon Sinek, calls it "your why." The famous motivational speaker, Les Brown, calls it "your drive." I describe it as being a problem-solver.

Performing high-quality work or offering first-class services requires that you become excellent in whatever you do.

Management consultant and author, Peter Drucker—considered to be the father of management—highly recommended that you decide to become "an effective executive."

"But I am not an executive," you might say. I used to say the same thing until Peter Drucker's teaching opened my eyes.

In his book, *The Effective Executive*, he defined an executive this way: "Every knowledge worker in modern organization is an 'executive' if, by virtue of his position or knowledge, he is responsible for a contribution that materially affects the capacity of the organization to perform and to obtain results."

So, you are an executive. You should strive to be an excellent one instead of a hardworking, zealous, busy and average one. But at what cost?

The price

As best-selling author and cartoonist, Scott Adams, puts it in his book, *How to Fail at Almost Everything and Still Win Big*: "One of the best pieces of advice I've ever heard goes something like this: If you want success, figure out the price, then pay it. It sounds trivial and obvious, but if you unpack the idea it has extraordinary power."

For instance, among many things, choosing to be excellent and to work with a sense of purpose means to systematically

- Lead with grace and integrity that inspires others.
- Do work worth talking about—work your *boss* can take credit for.
- Read or study the fine print others don't care about.

Creating winning career systems

- Think for yourself—instead of following the crowd.
- Take on the hard work that most employees won't do.
- Put in 20 hours when most colleagues put in 10.
- Accomplish more than you are asked.
- Commit to doing quality work for yourself, your company and the customers who are dying for better services.
- Care for customers' needs and satisfaction.

Therefore, it's crucial to think about what you enjoy doing and are good at so you can serve the world with no regret and resentment.

The benefits

In October 1967, less than a year before Dr. Martin Luther King, Jr., was killed, he traveled to Pennsylvania to speak to a group of high schoolers. There, he delivered his famous speech, "What's Your Life's Blueprint?" and offered some of the best career advice of all times, which no underdog can afford to ignore.

Dr. King said that foremost you must have "...the determination to achieve excellence in your various fields of endeavor." He elaborated by saying that once you decide what field to go into, you should "set out to do it, and to do it well."

Professionals have a critical decision to make about their careers. They can choose their life's work or let others control their career by dictating the kind of work they can do.

The choice to let others dictate looks easy, but it is costly and frustrating at best. No risk, no responsibility, but no rewards and no personal fulfillment either!

In his speech to the high schoolers in Pennsylvania, Dr. King quoted Ralph Waldo Emerson: "If a man can write a better book or preach a better sermon or make a better mousetrap than his neighbor, even if he builds his house in the woods, the world will make a beaten path to his door."

As I ponder Ralph Waldo Emerson's quote, I realize many people struggle to find space in the crowded job market, but the market creates room for those who refuse to be average.

Committing to pursuing excellence and doing work with purpose is one thing, but how you get there is a different ball game. So, where do you start? What are the strategies that will get you there? What resources do you need?

The upcoming chapters will address these questions. Let's start with the fundamentals: your job versus your work.

Reflection questions

- How am I leading?
- Am I working with a sense of purpose?
- Who do I do my best work for?
- What should I improve on right now to approach my work more systematically?

CHAPTER 2

Your Work vs. Your Job

Your job title and what you do for a living are not the same thing. I am grateful to Seth Godin for this eye-opening insight. This is one of the many career lessons I learned from his books.

To be blunt, you can't become remarkable if you fail to understand the difference between your job and your work.

- What's your title?
- What do you do?
- Who do you really work for?
- What problem do you solve?
- What kind of change do you make?

There's a business I could use 3 minutes from my house, but I drive 15 minutes to a different location. Why? Because my experience at the closer one has been terrible. I dread going there because most of the staff are mean, grumpy and bluntly condescending.

Like most average workers, the staff applied for and got jobs they don't even want to do. Worse, they have no interest in understanding the nature of their jobs now that they have them. Understanding the job you signed up for and what it requires is critical to your success if you want to catch the attention of your customers and employers, and earn their respect and admiration. More importantly, your job should match your life's work.

Unfortunately, lots of good employees, folks with good intentions, can't figure out the difference between their jobs and their work and fail to understand and master their life's work. Consequently, they get stuck in jobs they hate.

The difference...

Your employer owns your job, but you own your work. Simple. You take your best work anywhere you want and get paid to keep doing it. But your job or job title belongs to your employer. And one day, sooner or later, you will walk away from it. If you are an excellent employee, your job or your job title is replaceable, but you and your best work should not be.

In 1985, Steve Jobs was pushed out of his job at the company he co-created. But he kept doing his best work and went on to create NeXT. As a result of his best work, he was brought back to Apple in 1987 when the company almost hit rock bottom. You and I know what Apple represents today thanks to Steve Jobs, don't we?

The world needs your best work, your craft and your art.

What accepting a job means

Keeping your promises to your employer reinforces your experience and position in the job market—which should also lead you closer to your career dreams.

> Accepting a job offer is a commitment to advancing the mission of your employer or to helping bring some elements of a solution to the problem being tackled. Doing anything less is missing the opportunity to stand out from the crowd.

Once you understand the difference between your job and your work, growing your career becomes more doable and less painful. To repeat Seth Godin, you have a calling to make a difference wherever you go. And this is the best way to break away from harsh competition.

A deadly career trap

Your colleagues might push for more authenticity and transparency. They want you to be open about everything. You might be tempted to speak your mind—get things off your chest.

However, refrain from shooting yourself in the foot. Failing to understand the true meaning of "being an authentic employee" in the workplace might wreck your career, sooner or later. Is that what you want?

Most professionals believe authenticity in the workplace means "be your true self," "do as you please," or "say what's on your mind." They, therefore, act based on that belief and run into trouble. They end up hurting their career and get labeled "not a team player."

By the time they realize the buzz words "transparency" or "authenticity" are traps, it's too late.

What is authenticity in a workplace context? Let's look at how Seth Godin defines authenticity.

"We call a brand or a person authentic when they're consistent, when they act the same way whether or not someone is looking. Someone is authentic when their actions are in alignment with what they promise."

But wait, there's more. Seth explains that for him, being authentic is about doing what you've promised rather than being "who you are."

Here's the bottom line: There are a million places where you can be your true self—but the workplace is not one of them. That is, your employer pays you to be consistent, keep your promises—and do your best work.

It does not matter whether you like your boss or not. It doesn't matter if you woke up on the wrong side of the bed. To be authentic is to be reliable and dependable.

It's delivering on promises you make in your employment contract until you resign and take your best work elsewhere.

What can underdogs and undervalued employees do?

Career Move #2 – Treat each job as an opportunity to refine your best work.

Doing your best work on the job should be your ultimate goal because you own your work, you are a brand by yourself and because you should keep your promises to your employer.

You owe it to yourself to do work that is remarkable, irreplaceable or non-duplicatable in a systematic way. Work that makes customers notice your absence. Work that encourages customers to choose your company over its competitors. Work that makes clients come back for more—because of you.

Like Dr. King would say: "Even if it falls your lot to be a street sweeper, go on out and sweep streets like Michelangelo painted pictures; sweep streets like Handel and Beethoven composed music…sweep streets like Shakespeare wrote poetry."

Your best work might take you far—farther than you could ever imagine.

Bettering your luck

Are you maximizing your job opportunity? What are you becoming on the job?

Your job, whether small or big, is not yours. But it offers a chance for you to build a brand, a reputation and a portfolio worth sharing or talking about at your next job interview. You can maximize the opportunity your job provides and use it as a path to bigger things…to a better job, to a higher salary…or to the creation of your business.

Take Albert Einstein, for example. After he graduated from college in 1900, he could not get a job for two years. Surprising, right?

You might say, "Wasn't Einstein a genius?" Yes, he was a brilliant man. But you forget one thing: most average hiring managers are not capable of identifying and recognizing raw talent and potential.

To increase his chance of getting a job, Einstein expanded his network of friends and acquaintances and asked for help. Fortunately, thanks to his friend's father, he got a job as an assistant examiner at the Federal Office for Intellectual Property.

Getting the job was one thing, but what Einstein did with it changed his life forever.

On the job, Einstein mastered machine technology and learned more about the transmission of electricity. He used the experience to ponder over questions related to electrodynamics and theoretical physics. Before long, he had moved on to become a lecturer at the University of Bern. Simply put, he used his job as a steppingstone to get to the next level.

What a job brings

In addition to getting you a paycheck, your job, small or big, does seven critical things:

- It offers you a chance to solve problems and do better things than you've done before.
- It gives you a chance to learn new skills and sharpen your ability.
- It allows you the opportunity to network and meet new people.
- It provides a way to create a personal brand and build a reputation.
- It is a platform to show the world what you are made of.
- It gives an opportunity to serve and help other people.
- It is an opportunity to be helpful, kind and generous, making the world a better place.

That's why doing your best work at all times is a critical strategy in your career blueprint. Otherwise, people will keep using you in their career strategies. As the American writer, futurist and businessman, Alvin Toffler, argued: "If you don't have a strategy, you are part of someone else's strategy."

But how can we use our job and work to get ahead? What should we focus on? We will discuss these questions in the next chapter.

Reflection questions

- How am I maximizing my job opportunity?
- Where can I volunteer to keep doing my best work? (That is, if I don't have a job now.)
- What are three things I can do to improve the quality of my lifework?
- What should I change right now before it's too late?

CHAPTER 3

A Highly Neglected Career Success Factor

They say, "Time is money." But this is misleading because all minutes are not created equal. Imagine how much money people like Jeff Bezos and Oprah Winfrey make per minute and you will understand.

Are you mishandling the small things—the small jobs? As the American writer, futurist and businessman Alvin Toffler said, "You've got to think about big things while you're doing small things, so that all the small things go in the right direction." That said, you've got to get your career priority right. See, there are employees. And then there are *valuable* employees. They don't get the same treatment in the marketplace. Their time is not worth the same.

Employers can quickly hire and replace average workers. It's no big deal. It happens every day. However, replacing an excellent employee—a valuable team member—is like looking for a needle in a haystack. Similarly, losing a valuable employee creates tension. It might even lead to the loss of businesses as soon as customers notice the gap in the company's services.

The design whisperer

In June 2019, Chief Design Officer, Jony Ive, announced that he resigned from Apple. But who is Jony Ive? Jony is the mastermind that designed the look of the iPhone, the iPad, the Apple Watch, the Mac and the iPod. In other words,

Jony does remarkable work, and the impact of his resignation was mind-boggling.

According to Mary Hanbury, a writer for *Business Insider*, Jony's resignation shocked many people, including analysts who described Jony as "irreplaceable" and said his departure would create a real gap in the company. Almost instantly after the announcement, Apple's stock dropped 0.87%, sinking Apple's market capital by $8 billion. It was like having a Bond movie without James Bond in it.

There is no doubt that valuable employees have a direct and indirect impact on a company's businesses, whether management acknowledges it or not. But smart bosses know it.

Hiring mistakes

All companies or businesses are built around human beings—valuable talents. Having nice buildings and furniture is appealing, but they do not generate profits or lead to success since they are far from being as valuable as human resources. From the beginning of time, businesses have relied on valuable staff to grow their fortune, and they will continue to do so.

Some hiring managers let power go to their heads and show a lack of respect for job candidates. Others pretend their companies run smoothly and have a great organizational culture. But don't let anyone fool you. Most of the time, they don't know what they don't know or don't have.

What's worse, hiring managers fail to identify potential and settle for average. So, don't beat yourself up when you get no job offers as quickly as you want. An example? Tom Brady, the six-time Superbowl champ, was a 199th overall draft pick in the National Football league. Most of the teams skipped him.

See, most often, employers settle for average employees because hiring managers don't know better. That's why crappy customer service, bad attitudes and low-quality products are everywhere we turn. As a result, these companies struggle to stay in business year after year without overcoming the competition and satisfying their employees.

It's a catch-22. Dissatisfied employees provide average customer services that hold companies in harsh competition, and these companies can't satisfy their staff because harsh competition eats up their budget—and profits. The bad news is this cycle won't end soon.

On the other hand, there is hope in the job market for valuable talents. Many employers need your remarkable work. They need talents that can create tension, drive innovation and move the needle.

Talents who can run with their vision and offer customers more than what they thought they needed. Working for these companies that need these kinds of excellent employees will raise your value even more.

What most employees get wrong

Now, you are probably thinking, "I need to become more valuable in the job market. But how?"

> You might be tempted to work harder. Or work long hours. Or keep yourself busy all the time, hoping it will make you loved, respected and influential. Unfortunately, this strategy does not work. For many years, I made this mistake and lost lots of opportunities.

Being busy leads to nothing as long as employers can replace you with an average worker. However, working smarter, solving interesting problems, standing out, and doing remarkable work is priceless.

It will get you noticed. By the way, you will never have enough hours to sell to make a decent living if you fail to increase your value in the marketplace.

What can underdogs and undervalued employees do?

Career Move #3 - Perform work or tasks that increase your value.

The secret is, as the great speaker and motivator, Jim Rhon, said, "You don't get paid for the hour. You get paid for the value you bring to the hour."

What does it mean to increase your value? It means doing this:

- Continuously sharpen your skills, expand your knowledge, learn to solve interesting problems and be as consistent and excellent as possible in your field.
- Search for and take on challenges that most colleagues don't want to deal with.
- Repeat the words of the famous comedian, Steve Martin, to yourself: "Be so good they can't ignore you."

Doing quality work consistently and systematically makes you reliable and dependable. It has nothing to do with the number of hours you put in; it depends on how you help move the company's mission and vision forward.

By committing to being excellent and valuable—or a linchpin—you automatically raise yourself above the competition. It's your way of sending a clear message that you care about doing remarkable work—which means you will be putting customers and employers first on the road to building a fulfilling and rewarding career for yourself.

The more valuable you become, the more irreplaceable you will be. Why? Valuable talents are like gold. Companies like to hire and keep them. Without them, companies are already doomed. It's just a matter of time before they throw in the towel.

The key to becoming valuable

Jim Rhon revealed the secret to a successful career in one single sentence: "Work harder on yourself than you do on your job."

That's right. The best way to do excellent or better work is to better yourself. For instance:

- Establish a system to manage your time and energy. (Do this first!)
- Focus on using your time and energy to learn new stuff, develop new skills and solve interesting problems instead of going with the flow or fitting in.
- Chase and take on challenges others avoid.

And above all, be consistent in your performance on the job.

What does energy have to do with it?

Everything! Here are some examples:

- Oprah Winfrey said, "Energy is the essence of life. Every day you decide how you're going to use it by knowing what you want and what it takes to reach that goal, and by maintaining focus."
- Scott Adams described personal energy as "anything that gives you a positive lift, either mentally or physically." He added, "Generous people take care of their own needs first. In fact, doing so is a moral necessity. The world needs you at your best."
- The former pro football player, Ralph Marston, said that you should "put your energy into building what is creative, valuable and empowering. And you won't have to constantly fight against what is destructive and draining."
- The public speaker, life coach and philanthropist, Anthony Robbins, explained, "The higher your energy level, the more efficient your body. The more efficient your body, the better you feel and the more you will use your talent to produce outstanding results."

Spending energy on the wrong things is a terrible mistake. "It takes too much energy to be against something unless it's really important," argued author, Madeleine L'Engle.

In addition, the actress, businesswoman and singer Eva Gabor shared, "I learned early that you only have so much energy to give. You have to spend it correctly." I should have learned this in my 20's, but I was too busy being busy. So, I missed the point.

What's my point?

- Spend your energy on the tasks that matter the most for your career.
- Work on challenging projects that will raise your profile.
- As Jim Rohn said, "Don't major in minor things."

How energy management affects performance

Most professionals do not know how to allocate and spend their personal energy. Therefore, they have no significant achievements to show for their hard work.

Anyone who wants to hold you back just needs to do one thing: waste your energy on work that does not matter. Or keep you busy being busy. In 2019, the Toronto Raptors won the NBA finals over the Golden State Warriors.

Here's how. The Raptors' primary strategy was to make the Warriors' star player, Steph Curry, spend all his energy moving and relocating on the court. And it worked.

Kevin O'Connor of *The Ringer* reported, "Curry was exhausted by the fourth quarter, and appeared frustrated by the special attention the Raptors gave him, often grimacing or hanging his head."

They "wear him down physically until it affects his mind. The physical fatigue led to mental fatigue, resulting in sloppy decisions," added O'Connor.

You waste your energy, you lose.

Coach Bill Belichick of the New England Patriots is a master at making his opponents waste their energy. That's why he is the greatest coach in NFL history, with eight Super Bowl rings under his belt.

"What's Belichick's best strategy?" you might ask. His team runs long drives or keeps the ball for a long time. This way, he forces his opponents to spend their energy on defense until their players get exhausted—and start making bad decisions.

The bottom line is, there's no way to become a valuable talent if you let other people control how you spend your daily dose of energy. Instead, you ought to be intentional in how you manage your energy. As Scott Adams said, "Your mind isn't magic. It's a moist computer you can program. The most important metric to track is your personal energy."

Therefore, spending personal energy on training and developing better skill sets is a smart move. But what kind of training? This leads us to the next chapter: employee training.

Reflection questions

- Am I aware of how I spend my energy at work?
- Who controls my time?
- How do I pick tasks that increase my value?
- What can I do to manage my time and energy more systematically?

Coach Teddy Edouard

CHAPTER 4

Most Employee Training Sessions Aren't for Employees

What are you becoming on the job? How effective and practical is the training support you are getting? How are you learning your job?

There are different types of employee professional development opportunities, and they are not created equal. For example, there's in-house training (traditional training), external training (purchased from vendors) and training funds (and tuition reimbursement) for staff members to pay for courses they want as long as the course aligns with their jobs.

Getting funds to pay for your own training is an excellent professional development (PD) opportunity since it allows you to pick courses to fill your skills and competency gaps. If you are lucky, your boss might let you take classes to prepare for your next career move.

Unfortunately, most employers offer only traditional training. They tend to claim they don't have the budget to finance employee's PD. If you find yourself in this situation, get ready to deal with lots of irrelevant and boring training sessions. I already feel your pain because I have been there.

Traditional training

What I am saying is, you might think employers know how to train, lead and increase employee performance. But think again. In October 2019, Steve Glaveski, CEO and co-founder of Collective Campus, a consulting firm, wrote an article titled "Where Companies Go Wrong with Learning and

Development" in the *Harvard Business Review*. In his article, he took a critical look at the effectiveness of corporate training.

> Let's be blunt here. Like most companies, your employer might need training on how to run effective training to create a learning culture that leads to high performance. If your employer isn't good at providing effective training, where does that leave you when you rely on in-house training to improve your skills?

Steve specifically discussed the return on the $359 billion budget organizations worldwide spent on training in 2016. Let me share with you the list he came up with:

- 75% of 1,500 managers surveyed from across 50 organizations were dissatisfied with their company's Learning & Development (L&D) function;
- 70% of employees report that they don't have mastery of the skills needed to do their jobs;
- Only 12% of employees apply new skills learned in L&D programs to their jobs; and
- Only 25% of respondents to a recent McKinsey survey believe that training measurably improved performance.

The very department in charge of employee learning fails to understand how learning or skill development works. Isn't that alarming?

> See, trusting your employer with your learning—your career development—is like asking a struggling stockbroker to show you how to beat the market. So, relying on employers to help you become the best at what you do will never work. In this case, you are more likely to be the victim of your high expectations.

The issue is that the root causes of mediocre or ineffective employee training lie in how companies and managers view training and learning. "What do you mean?" you wonder.

Scary training and learning stories

I was tasked to work with a manager on improving the quality of training products for hundreds of people, and we started with a bunch of dreadful PDF training documents.

After reviewing the documents, I realized there was too much filler or unnecessary content. So, I recommended we remove the filler, break the content into step-by-step instructions with case studies and comprehension questions, and sequence the modules in a way that would facilitate better understanding. My suggestions also included ideas to make learning interactive, facilitate knowledge transfer, and cut the training time in half.

To my surprise, the manager said no to the proposed changes. She added that we should not make things easier for employees because it's their job to learn whatever the company asks them to learn since they are getting paid for it.

Another training manager asked me to create a tutorial that would help end-users navigate a tool with fewer mistakes. I reviewed the tool and realized it was very confusing. Even worse, I checked with the manager and observed that even he had issues explaining how to navigate the tool. I proposed we make the tool simpler and more user friendly. We could test it and try to refine it with user input. But the response I got was, "Sorry, we don't have time for that now. Employees will just have to deal with it."

It's also common to hear managers complaining that employees attend training but still make mistakes. Or managers send the staff back to remediation or more training because the staff makes mistakes, as though training has a magic power to solve systemic performance issues. I could go on and *on* with my horror stories about employee training, but I think you get the point: there is a lot of ineffective training out there.

A distorted view of training and learning

My colleagues in the learning and development field have made the same observations over and over. I agreed with Steve Glaveski when he said, "Not only is the majority of training in today's companies ineffective, but the purpose, timing, and content of training is flawed."

Most institutions or training departments (or whatever we call them) operate under the assumption that learning is a simple task employees should complete at once because it's their job to do so.

Therefore, lots of employers could not care less about the quality of their training sessions or the effectiveness of their learning culture since they believe they already do employees a favor by giving them a job. That leads us to a sad reality.

The hidden purpose of most employee training...

Could companies do better in the area of training and development? Yes, they could. But do they want to? Here's the sad reality:

- Most training sessions are based on a lie. They make false learning-and-performance-improvement promises. On top of that, they often waste employees' time and energy.
- Most training sessions are there to cover management's back. They enable managers and supervisors to check the box, claiming they are promoting learning. That way, it's easy to blame employees for performance issues—or a company's systematic and leadership shortcomings—instead of taking on the responsibility to build systems that promote peak performance and growth.

In other words, most sessions you attend are not designed for your learning or benefit. Instead, they are a way for leadership to hide instead of lead.

Creating winning career systems

As Bill Belichick said, "Good players can't overcome bad coaching."

Thus, no amount of training will compensate for ineffective management systems and flawed organizational culture. So, if you are serious about mastering your job or becoming the best at what you do, you will need your own learning system.

What can underdogs and undervalued employees do?

Career Move #4 – Take charge of your learning now.

As we just discussed, most employers, intentionally or unintentionally, fail to establish systems to promote effective and practical training and knowledge transfer, let alone career development opportunities. Some might also believe if they train you well, you will leave.

Most big shots in leadership positions have their coaches or consultants—but they are totally fine with sending employees to training or PD courses. Isn't that interesting?

Let's hope you are not expecting employers to help you to learn your job. Because putting your learning in employers' hands is like playing at a casino with your income and hoping to retire with millions in the bank.

Take the wheel.

You have no choice but to take charge of your career development, career trajectory and career destiny. To be successful at this, here are seven things you need to do:

- Understand that effective career development will require extra effort on your part.
- Avoid relying on employers for your training and learning unless you just want to learn to meet basic standards and expectations—and let your job go to waste.
- Attend training. But keep in mind you will forget most of what you learned from your training before you even

get back on the job. Often, the training will have nothing to do with the tasks you perform on the job. See the challenge?
- Build relationships with colleagues, observe them and ask for help. In other words, find opportunities for guided practice and collaboration where you can make mistakes safely.
- Get all the advice you can, but do your homework, paying attention to details and reading the fine points.
- Find your own training and invest in your career.
- Search for informal or formal coaching support that can help you develop your skills and competencies.

You give yourself an edge when you go the extra mile to increase your knowledge and sharpen your skills. How so? Because most employees attend training when they are asked to, not because they want to focus on being the best.

The next chapter addresses professional development in a more systematic way. Let's move on to continue this conversation.

Reflection questions

- Have I identified my skill gaps?
- What kind of learning opportunities will help fill these gaps?
- What kind of informal learning should I be doing?
- What learning decision should I take now before it's too late?

CHAPTER 5

The Quintessential Move for Career Success

How sharp are your learning skills? What learning strategies do you use? As Alvin Toffler said, "The illiterate of the 21st century will not be those who cannot read and write, but those who cannot learn, unlearn, and relearn." There are career goals. And there are professional development (PD) systems. They are not the same. Here's why…

- Setting goals might get you a job but creating a professional/personal growth-oriented system will give you a successful career—or make you an irreplaceable asset.
- Pursuing stand-alone goals is limited. Unless you have a personal development system that *consistently* increases your knowledge, ability and performance, you won't escape competition and earn the respect you deserve.
- Having an effective professional/personal development system enables underdogs like us to embark on a continuous improvement (CI) journey to get better day by day and week after week.
- Building a PD system is a commitment to take small but consistent learning steps that lead to expertise and superior skills that are beyond the scope and reach of employee training.

Like they say, "Goals win games, but systems win championships."

What outliers do

Outliers are professionals who outperform almost everyone to eventually reach Hall of Fame status in their field or their sports. Outliers capitalize on the effectiveness of systems to transform themselves into elite performers that stand out in the crowd. Want examples?

- There are many good orators. And then there are Barack Obama, Dr. Martin Luther King, Jr., Wilson Churchill and Abraham Lincoln.
- The NFL has many excellent quarterbacks. And then there are Tom Brady and Joe Montana. There are great football coaches and then there are Bill Belichick, Bill Parcells, Don Shula and Bill Walsh.
- The National Basketball Association (NBA) has great coaches. And then there is Phil Jackson. The NBA has lots of star players, and then there are Michael Jordan, Lebron James and Steph Curry.
- There are many outstanding pop singers. And then there is Michael Jackson. There are many heavyweight boxers, and then there are Mike Tyson, Rocky Marciano and Mohammed Ali.
- There are plenty of good scientists. And then there are Albert Einstein, Marie Curie, Isaac Newton and Nikola Tesla.
- There are plenty of successful rappers. And then there is Jay Z. Plenty of remarkable female tennis players, and then there are Serena Williams and Naomi Osaka. Plenty of superb soccer players, and then there are Pele, Maradona, Romario, Messi, Ronaldo and Ronaldinho. There are many great baseball players, and then there are Babe Ruth, Jackie Robinson and Mickey Mantle.

These outliers have one thing in common. Undoubtedly, they have a way (a system) to perform at a higher level than their competitors. They do things in a way that sets them apart from the crowd.

They don't have a perfect record, but they have an edge—a system. They are, in what they do, almost as consistent as the seasons of the year. And this is the holy grail of systems. Systems bring consistency that helps ordinary people achieve extraordinary things.

What can underdogs and undervalued employees do?

Career Move #5 – Develop personal development systems instead of stand-alone goals.

> You need an effective and personalized PD system that will equip you to outlearn, outperform and outsmart your competitors until you escape harsh competition in the job market. A system has and will always be the best way to the top. "But what is a system?" you may ask. Let me explain:

- In his book, *How to Lose at Almost Everything and Still Win Big*, Scott Adams describes it this way: "In the world of dieting, losing twenty pounds is a goal, but eating right is a system. In the exercise realm, running a marathon in under four hours is a goal, but exercising daily is a system. In business, making a million dollars is a goal, but being a serial entrepreneur is a system."
- Reading a book about your field of work is a goal, but reading regularly and staying up-to-date and informed about new developments in your field is a system.
- Taking courses to renew a license or certification is a goal, but reading new research, learning new skills and presenting at conferences is a system that will keep you sharp.

"A system is something you do on a regular basis that increases your odds of happiness in the long run. If you do something every day, it's a system. If you're waiting to achieve it someday in the future, it's a goal," said Scott Adams.

Using systems is a sure way to develop habits that last and make it possible for you to reach mastery. This is especially if you want to beat procrastination and your flagging willpower.

What your system should include

Your personal development system should, among many things, and depending on your needs, include some of the following:

- **Reading:** Time to read regularly about top performers and experts from a variety of fields. Read your way to power. According to Alvin Toffler, "Knowledge is the most democratic source of power."

- **Networking:** A way to regularly meet people you can learn from and who make you want to do better.

- **Skill Development:** Opportunities to practice skills regularly, get feedback and take corrective actions to develop and sharpen your skills and performance.

- **Communication:** A space to practice and get feedback to improve your communication skills and strategies.

- **Portfolio:** A way to create products, tools and artifacts that display skills and competencies you bring to the job market.

- **Presentations/Associations:** Spaces or conferences where you can test your skills, share your knowledge and learn from experts or leaders in your field of work.

- **Leadership:** Opportunities to lead, make decisions and solve interesting problems. The more problems you solve, the better you will get.

- **Coaching:** Guides to show you the way
- **Branding:** A way to shape and present your story to the world, sending a clear message about what you stand for and the kind of problems you help solve

Setting yourself on a successful career path is possible, but it requires time, energy and resources you might not have. However, finding the right kinds of help and advice will make things easier for you—or at least help you grow faster.

As I pointed out, most big shots in leadership positions have their coaches or consultants. They don't attend employee training. So, it's about time you took a page from their playbook.

Getting your own guide

A Chinese proverb says, "A single conversation with a wise man is better than ten years of study." Which wise man or woman have you been talking to?

That means you should join professional memberships that share your interests and get a coach to show you the way instead of relying only on your personal experience and boring training.

Working with a coach saves time, resources and lots of trouble figuring out insights and strategies you can access immediately.

Do you know champs who have no coach? Keep in mind, champs and linchpins work with coaches and mentors instead of spending time and energy on average training. Think about it. Olympic-level athletes can get only so good through their own efforts. To reach the pinnacle, they need a world-class coach.

Here's the ultimate secret: Getting a career coach will give you an edge over most competitors. How so? Most professionals don't even know they need one. Keep this between us.

By the way, getting a good coach is one of the fastest and best ways to reach mastery. Yes, you ought to master some skills—or something. Otherwise, you are a walking generality with nothing to separate yourself from the crowd.

Why don't we discuss mastery in the next chapter?

Reflection questions

- Do I understand how PD systems work?
- How can I build or reinforce my PD system?
- What do I need in my personalized PD system?
- What coaching needs do I have?
- What decisions about my PD system should I make today?

CHAPTER 6

A Talent Differentiator

What do you want to master? What are you known for? Your answer should show what makes you stand out in the job market. I did this type of career inventory and it helped me better position myself in the marketplace.

Simone Biles

With about thirty Olympic and World Champion medals in her treasure box—or wherever she keeps them—Simone Biles is a force to be reckoned with in the gymnastics world.

Being the most decorated American gymnast and the third most decorated in the world, it's obvious that Simone knows things and does things that average gymnasts do not.

How did she win so many medals? She mastered the sports to the point that even gravity seems to bow down to her physical and mental agility and toughness.

But what most people don't know is that her level of mastery results from hard work. For example, in 2012, it was reported that Simone Biles trained for about 32 hours weekly. That's like working a full-time job. No wonder she is that good.

TD Jakes

There are preachers, and then there's Bishop Thomas Dexter Jakes, Sr. – known as TD Jakes. The man from West Virginia is a prolific writer, filmmaker and Grammy Award winner. Named one of the top 10 religious leaders in America, the founder of the Potter's House in Dallas, Texas, is one of the most influential spiritual figures in the world. But what makes TD Jakes so prominent and respected?

Most people who hear him preach can tell he has a wealth of knowledge of the Bible, he has mastered the art of public speaking, and he excels in storytelling. He also makes Bible verses come alive using vivid illustrations and imagery that reflect everyday life.

It goes without saying that he is a hardworking pastor who has mastered his art. He spends time studying his craft, preparing his sermons and working on his calling. He can't be as good as he is by accident.

Marie Callender

You can bake, but not as well as Marie Callender. She and her husband started baking pies in her home kitchen in the 1930s. She sold them to shops and restaurants—then an exciting thing happened. Demand for the pies skyrocketed.

Marie Callender became a national chain—a famous brand name. She turned her kitchen-based, pie-baking business into a multimillion-dollar company. But how was it possible for her to make a million dollars baking pies?

Well, there are pies, and then there are *delicious* pies. We both know they are not the same! Marie's secret was in her mastery. She worked hard to master the art of making and baking pies, and creating her own recipes. And the world made room and space for her because the marketplace is always looking for better.

Chris Garner

Chris Garner is a well-known businessman and public speaker with an inspiring story. In the Navy, he learned a lot about laboratory and surgical techniques and started a career in the medical field. But then he abandoned his dream to become a physician and do the unexpected.

He became an excellent stockbroker instead. The movie, *The Pursuit of Happyness,* shows the ordeals, such as homelessness, that Garner faced before reaching a level of success in his career. Today, the man who used to be homeless is helping to create housing opportunities for low-income families in San Francisco. Inspiring, right?

But how did he reach this level of success?

Garner got an opportunity as a trainee at Dean Witter Reynolds and leveraged it to climb to the next level. He outworked, outstudied and outperformed everyone, stopping at nothing to pass his exams with gusto.

Garner went on to work for **Bear Stearns & Company** in San Francisco. He mastered stock trading, and the stock market welcomed him with open arms.

What mastery means

Steve Martin summarized the concept of mastery in one sentence: "Be so good that you can't be ignored." But what does "be so good" mean?

The previous stories show that "be so good" means developing one's raw skills and talents in a systematic way to reach a level of excellence that nears perfection. It's the act of crossing the border into "The Land of Excellence," leaving behind an overwhelmingly crowded and competitive place filled with people longing to get in but without a ship to get there.

Performing at a level of excellence is the line that separates amateurs from pros, average employees from linchpins, and so-called leaders from guides and talent builders. Simply put, it's what separates the Elon Musks and Mohammed Alis of the world from the average person.

"Be so good" means having the capacity to make greater and better things–work that changes people and companies for the good and contributions that make people miss you when you are gone.

Seth Godin explains that making things better and doing world-class work make you visible to others. That's because people like to feel recognized for having good taste or for spotting important ideas. Your outstanding work makes it easy for people to talk about you because they think talking about your work says something about themselves.

Nowadays, most professionals want special recognition for meeting standard expectations. But in the kingdom of excellent performers, as the international public speaker and writer, Jon Petz, said, "Meeting expectations is like doing nothing all." Thus, to "be so good" is to position yourself as an outlier. It's breaking the limits and boundaries of basic expectations. Consequently, in a world where most talents get by on surface knowledge, function on autopilot, and just meet standard expectations, you are choosing to be invisible if you choose the same path. Is that what you really want?

What can underdogs and undervalued employees do?

Career Move #6 – Dedicate time and energy to master your work (or your field).

Reaching mastery is your only option to becoming visible and setting yourself apart from the crowd. You must do quality work that catches people's attention. So, establishing a system to pursue mastery is a smart professional move.

The job market is saturated with "average." Therefore, average performance is boring and indistinguishable. As Seth Godin said, "The only way to get what you're worth is to stand out, to exert emotional labor, to be seen as indispensable…"

Mastery is key to your success, but it requires a high level of focus. It's not for the weak, the faint of heart and the distracted. As the famous American author, Robert Greene, said, "The time that leads to mastery is dependent on the intensity of our focus." Are you ready to put in the work?

> Focusing on mastery is the best way to create your future. Unless you make it your priority, the job market will shape your future without your permission. Who would like that?

But how do you reach mastery?

The road to mastery

To repeat the famous Japanese, Chef Jiro, "You must immerse yourself in your work. You have to fall in love with your work... You must dedicate your life to mastering your skill. That's the secret of success." But there's a hiccup. The road to mastery passes through risks and failures. Thus, understanding failure and learning to fail well is critical to your success.

So, start by learning to fail as often as possible. And your best learning will come from your ability to fail, bounce back and keep moving forward.

As Robert Greene explains in his book, *Mastery*, there are two kinds of failure. The first comes from not even trying due to fear or because you think the timing's not quite right. But he says this is the kind of failure you never learn from and that can crush you.

The second kind of failure, Green says, "comes from a bold and venturesome spirit. If you fail in this way, the hit that you take to your reputation is greatly outweighed by what you learn." Rather than crushing you, Greene says that this kind of failure will toughen your resolve and give you a clear vision of how things need to be done.

A great way to learn mastery is to learn from the pros. How? Read books, listen to podcasts and get coaches or mentors. Find a way to get intentional practice and corrective feedback on your performance from someone who knows the way.

Concrete actions

In addition to using a personal development system as I described in Chapter 5, you should do the following:

- Be proactive in identifying gaps in your skills and knowledge.
- Make time for intentional, distraction-free practices.
- Learn to get in a "flow state" (a high-performance zone).
- Conduct distraction-free observations.
- Increase your level of attention and focus.
- Work on your biases (use an outsider perspective).
- Seek out relevant blogs and podcasts.
- Ask for advice and recommendations.
- Learn from the best of the best.
- Pay attention to details, learn to see clearly and identify trends and patterns.
- Take risks and execute your ideas.

Warning! When you get exhausted and feel like quitting, like I often feel, keep in mind that the road to mastery is also the highway to the future. And I don't think you want to miss the future.

Does work experience lead to mastery? It all depends. Let's talk about it in the upcoming chapter.

Reflection questions

- What are the skills or competencies you should master?
- Who are the best in the field, or who is leading the way?
- Who can help or coach me?
- What resources do I need?
- How much time should I dedicate to this learning process?
- What actions should I take today?

CHAPTER 7

A Common Career Misconception

Most people misunderstand work experience. Or better said, they take it for what it is not. Honestly, I did, too, for many years. I will elaborate.

Imagine you are recruiting for a project and need to select from two resumes. Applicant 1 has five years of experience versus Applicant 2 who has 15 years in the field. Who should you hire?

Let's hope you did not choose the person with 15 years of experience. Why? If you did, you just made the mistake that most hiring managers make. This is the kind of miscalculation that hurts both companies and talented professionals and eventually leads to stagnation across the board.

> The assumption that a candidate with 15 years of experience is more qualified or has more expertise than the one with five years of experience is misleading at best. Indeed, 15 years of experience looks good on paper. But in reality, it might also mean that the person has followed the same routine over and over again for 15 years without making adjustments and changes.

Simply put, years of experience don't always equate with expertise and mastery. In other words, experience and expertise are not the same.

Fifteen years of experience might mean working for fifteen years without seeking to sharpen and increase one's knowledge and skills. Contrastingly, a professional with five years of experience might have worked intentionally and consistently to innovate, expand her knowledge and improve her performance and abilities.

For example, having 35 years of driving experience does not qualify you to chauffer the U.S. President. "Why not?" you ask.

POTUS's chauffeur is an expert driver. People who drive for a president specialize in driving around dignitaries and their high-level security, and they have worked continuously to keep their skills as sharp as a razor.

So, is work experience valuable?

Yes, indeed. In fact, some experts have a lot of experience. But their experience alone does not make them the expert they are. Unlike average workers with adequate skills who perform tasks on autopilot, experts and excellent employees are outliers who focus on getting better day after day.

In other words, excellent professionals continuously look for ways to optimize their decision-making processes and performance.

Don't let years of work experience fool you.

The greatest NFL coach of all time never played in the league. How is that even possible? Many believe only players can become great coaches, right? But that is a mistake. Players tend to see games or game decision-making from the angle of the position they used to play.

The most famous, inexperienced employees in the world are first-term U.S. Presidents. They can only view the scope of and learn the job while doing it.

Sadly, experienced professionals rarely create innovative or world-changing companies. Don't believe me? Look at the following:

- Google, Tesla, Uber, PayPal, Apple, Microsoft, Facebook, Amazon and SpaceX all took novice and innovative minds to push the frontier of technology and navigate an ocean of limitations to bring them to life.
- Jeff Bezos, the founder of Amazon, challenged brick-and-motor stores and put numerous companies out of business as a first-time CEO. And many young CEOs continue the trend.
- Barack Obama went to Washington, D.C. as a first-term senator in 2005 and what he did next changed the course of history. As a newbie, he accomplished the unthinkable: he defeated the respected Senator Hillary Clinton, the Maverick John McCain and the famous businessman, Mitt Romney.
- Donald J. Trump, with no political experience, entered the presidential race and won the Republican nomination and the presidential election in 2016 by defeating the Washington insider and respected Secretary of State, Hillary Clinton. In doing so, he redefined the game of politics and changed what the media thought they knew about U.S. politics.

A blessing and a curse

> Experience gives professionals a blindside. In other words, it's hard for a manager with 25 years of experience to learn new strategies or insights about processes and procedures he believes he has mastered—or at least has been doing over and over for 25 years.

But there is more. Institutional and field knowledge can make things worse for experienced professionals. Why? Because they tend to be also a victim of the curse of knowledge. "What's the curse of knowledge?" you may ask.

Professionals with the curse of knowledge normalize or downplay their knowledge to the point that they believe everyone should know what they know or believe what they believe.

American author, Chip Heath, says that when you have the curse of knowledge, "it is impossible to imagine what it's like to lack that knowledge."

The worse problems? Having experience and knowledge but not having the ability to communicate and apply them effectively to innovate is a significant hindrance. Peter Thiel, author of *Zero to One*, said, "Today's 'best practices' lead to dead ends; the best paths are new and untried."

Getting stuck in the past or in one's experience gets in the way of progress, growth and innovation. It causes stagnation because, as Peter Drucker would argue, knowledge and experience alone can't lead to concrete results and achievements. But effectiveness can.

What can underdogs and undervalued employees do?

Career Move #7 – Learn from experienced people but always question limitations.

Many people will use their experience to make you feel that you do not measure up. They destroy your confidence, put you down and manipulate you. Of course, that makes them feel good. But they can't you keep down if you know what to do.

Thomas Edison did it to his employee, Nikola Tesla. Edison used his brilliance and experience to try to crush Tesla's dreams and career. But Tesla worked hard, developed business partnerships and launched an alternative current (AC) electricity business.

Here's what you should do:
- Pay close attention to what the linchpins (the best brains) in your companies do and learn as much as you can from them—except their limitations.

- Avoid building experience that protects and maintains the status quo.
- Test yourself, create your own way of doing things and drive your own change. More importantly, take charge of the trajectory of your career.

For example, the pro basketball player, Lebron James, left Cleveland Cavaliers for Miami Heat to win his first NBA championship ring. The pro basketball player, Kevin Durant, won his by joining the Golden State Warriors. Many in the media criticized these players' career moves.

But the detractors failed to understand that having a championship ring in the NBA or NFL looks much better than having a long career without winning a championship.

Shoot your best shots.

That said, you should make moves that are similar to winning championships, as opposed to accumulating years of work experience just for the sake of saying "I have experience." How? After building an effective PD system, you should use it to do the followings:

- Lead and inspire others.
- Focus on building a track record that speaks for itself.
- Study the market and know your stuff.
- Avoid getting traps by imposed limitations.
- Build a portfolio worth talking about.
- Work on big projects.
- Take on challenges and risks to solve real problems.
- Bring more solutions than issues to the marketplace.
- Don't wait for permission to do your best work.
- Make major contributions.

Since we're talking about significant contributions, let's elaborate on the topic in the next chapter.

Reflection questions

- Who are the leaders in my field?
- What are the limitations or challenges?
- What can I do to discover the secrets of the field or the market?
- What are the root causes that everybody seems to miss?
- What can I bring to the table to make my boss look good?

CHAPTER 8

The Art of Contribution

See, think, do.

- What do you bring to the table?
- What problems do you solve?
- Will you be missed when you are gone?
- What secrets do you have?

Here's how things go. Jane Doe sees a job announcement. She applies and gets the job. Of course, Jane Doe wants a paycheck, benefits and job satisfaction. But what does Jane Doe plan to bring to the table? Or in the words of the father of modern management, Peter Drucker, what contribution does she plan to make to the company's mission, projects and success?

Identifying the contribution you bring to the job market provides a clearer view and understanding of your value. The more contributions you make, the more valuable you are.

Most companies do not recruit professionals just because they need people to warm up their seats, drink their coffee and use their bathrooms. Instead, they want people who get things done—by bringing ideas, answers and solutions to advance their mission.

> Getting things done is why all employees sign up. So, getting away with doing the bare minimum might seem easy and smart in the short term, but it has disastrous consequences on one's career in the long run.

As Peter Drucker explained it, "Commitment to contribution is commitment to responsible effectiveness. Without it, a man shortchanges himself, deprives his organization, and cheats the people he works with."

The thing is, there are small contributions and big ones that are worth talking about. Most of the time, staff is asked to work on small contributions while major ones stay under the control of a few big shots in management, like the Edisons of the world. What does that mean for the little guys like the Teslas of the world?

Making significant contributions requires going above and beyond one's job description and responsibilities. It means taking on challenges and doing one's best work without asking for permission. Otherwise, one is stuck at the bottom of the career ladder forever.

Senator Obama in Illinois

The story goes like this. When former senator, Barack Obama, got elected in the senate in Illinois, he was determined to make a difference and to get ahead. But he ran into the status quo.

He built connections, did his homework and looked for opportunities to contribute—looked for gaps in the line of defense of the establishment. Sure enough, he found a few. How so?

A friend introduced the young senator to the godfather. The godfather? Yes, you read that right. Back then, Senator Emil Jones, the president of the Illinois Senate, was the most influential politician in the state. Obama knew that and put his skills and knowledge at his service. He volunteered to take on legislative tasks Emil Jones wanted done.

For Senator Obama, getting this opening was like a backup quarterback getting to play in a playoff game—or in the Superbowl game. So, he increased his contributions and his profile, broke away from the competition—and left behind those who wanted to maintain the status quo.

I believe Senator Obama's decision to focus on making contributions to improve the lives of Chicagoans might have been one of the most important moves—if not *the* most important move—the former senator made for his political career. Of course, Senator Obama made the godfather look good. In return, Senator Jones let Obama use his shoulders to get to the next level of his political career.

The godfather's blessing likely helped pave the way, send a signal, and open doors for his protégé to win a seat in the U.S. Senate and become the leader of the free world for eight years. And that leads me to the main point of this chapter.

What can underdogs and undervalued employees do?

Career Move #8 – Make major contributions to send a strong message to the job market.

What do people say about you on the job? What are you known for in the marketplace? Are you hiding, or are you leading from behind?

- You have a reputation, whether you build it yourself or not. Put differently, if you don't build the reputation you desire, the marketplace will give you one you might not like. So, you are better off taking risks to create your own—and have it your way, just like the former senator did in Illinois.
- You can make a reputation by causing trouble and fighting change. Or you act as a game-changer, playmaker or trailblazer. It's totally up to you. Yes, becoming a talent that helps build the future with innovative thinking, connections and by working smart takes hard work—but it's also rewarding.
- Therefore, your job is an opportunity to generate ideas, create products and make decisions that will make your boss look great; this will advance your employer's

mission and make competitors wish they had you on their team.

What contributions look like...

> Key contributions go beyond job expectations and surpass minimum performance standards. Therefore, doing what the crowd does will not cut it. Why? Because the crowd is satisfied with average performance and you should not be.

Contributions may vary depending on the jobs at hand, but they are hard to achieve. They are the challenges most colleagues want to avoid. The difficult tasks nobody wants to take on. The answers or information most people don't have. The products that require time and extra work to complete. Or the solution to lingering problems that keep management awake at night.

Excellent contributions make it easier for the boss to talk about you—or herself indirectly. In case you did not know, supervisors enjoy talking about their best recruits. Why? Because it's a way for them to show off and to tell colleagues that they know how to hire excellent staff—how to pick winners and linchpins. So, go ahead and do your boss a favor. Offer her a reason to say, "I hired___(add your name)__."

Where to start...

You can't contribute to work, projects or missions you don't understand well. Otherwise, you run the risk, like so many employees, of getting frustrated.

That will also cause you to misspend your time, resources and energy. Therefore, you need guidelines in your PD system on how to approach new jobs and work on the fundamentals.

For example, you need to

- Know thyself and thy boss (top priorities).

- Study your work context (the political system and the key players).
- Identify opportunities and restrictions.
- Know thy field of work.
- Identify the influencers of your field.
- Identify significant trends, challenges and shifts.
- Read case studies and breakthroughs.
- Ask the questions in a diplomatic way that nobody is asking.
- Identify and learn from the changemakers of your company.

Once you cover the fundamentals, start focusing on your personal development plan. Look for mentorship and coaching support that will help you learn fast, understand your company's culture and sharpen your skills. Then, start thinking about what kind of ideas, products and solutions—that is, what kind of contributions—you want to bring to the table.

The more solutions you bring, the better your contributions and the stronger your influence will be on the job. So, focusing on real problems and their root causes is crucial. For more on that, let's go to the next chapter.

Reflection questions

- Since all institutions are built on secrets, what are the secrets of my company?
- What are its pain points? What keeps management awake at night?
- Who runs the show and who are the gatekeepers? Who do I need to meet?
- What kind of support does my boss need to do her job?
- From whom should I learn?
- On what contributions should I be working?

Creating winning career systems

CHAPTER 9

Opportunity in the Noise

See, think, do.

- What opportunities do you see that others overlook?
- What company secrets do you personally have?
- How do you screen or select your information?

In the Gospel of Saint Matthew, Jesus's disciples complained they could not understand him because he spoke in parables to the crowd. He responded that the secret of his kingdom is not given to everyone and added, "This is why I speak to them in parables: Though seeing, they do not see; though hearing, they do not hear or understand."

This tells us looking is not seeing, and hearing is not understanding. With all the noise going on around us today, this could not be truer. Most professionals get by on having just enough information and knowledge. They act based on whatever watered-down, polished, fast-food information they can get. Most survive on "this is the way we have always done it" or on "best practices."

> Everyone is too busy, too behind and too bored to look closer and deeper. As a result, they fail to notice what's missing, what can be improved and where the root causes lie. Do you already see the opportunity?

An ocean of information and data

According to *Dazeinfo*, in 2000 there were 738 million mobile users in the world, but the number increased to 7 billion by the end of 2015. The smartphone of today is way more powerful than the computer NASA used in the 1960s to put a man on the moon. Today, a struggling factory worker with a smartphone in his pocket is more connected to the rest of the world than Martin Luther King, Jr., Abraham Lincoln, Alexander the Great, Julius Cesar, Napoleon Bonaparte, Jean Jacques Dessalines, Simon Bolivar and Winston Churchill could have ever been in their eras.

Most of the world should be grateful to technology during the COVID-19 pandemic. Technology has allowed us to remain connected with friends and family while practicing social distancing.

But progress in technology comes with a major setback: a flood of distractions that decrease attention, concentration and effectiveness. Television, social media and commercials overwhelmingly invade our daily life without our permission. We can't escape from screens! They are everywhere.

It's like most of us are drowning in a sea of information and hoping to swim fast enough to catch up and stay up to date. Sadly, catching up or keeping up is almost impossible. According to Domo.com, the Internet, social media, tech tools and companies produce on average about 2.5 quintillion bytes of data daily.

Problem and opportunity

Distractions, coupled with news bias, blindside most people—and decision-makers. Biases cripple decision-making power and judgment. Thus, we all face a problem and a great opportunity.

The problem? Distractions lead to mistakes, oversight and accidents. They decrease the ability of most people to think and see clearly. So, accepting and making decisions on fast-food information becomes a more accessible option.

The opportunity? Focus, concentration and analytical skills —"seeing skills"—are in high demand. Those who have a system for sorting out information, picking out the essentials, focusing, and thinking critically become the geniuses of the marketplace.

As Winston Churchill, the British Prime Minister during World War II, said, "True genius resides in the capacity for evaluation of uncertain, hazardous, and conflicting information." He should know.

> That said, those who can ignore the noise will lead the way in innovation, invention and transformation, thus helping to build a future they want and believe in.

Some examples…

Forty Second Boyd

Many Air Force fighter pilots flew on war missions and saw danger, challenges and death during those missions. But the famous American military strategist, John Boyd, saw an opening—an opportunity—to break away from traditional air combat maneuvering and war tactics. He invented the OODA Loop (*observe–orient–decide–act*), a process to make fast decisions to outsmart and outthink opponents.

John Boyd had the nickname "Forty Second Boyd" because he was so fast that he could defeat his opponents in 40 seconds. Today, he is known as one of the most brilliant military strategists of all time due to his ability to see beyond the obvious.

Chieko Asakawa

It was almost impossible for blind and visually impaired people to browse the internet. The Japanese computer scientist Chieko Asakawa saw the challenge and invented the Home Page Reader (HPR) in 1997.

This voice browser allows visually impaired folks to surf and navigate the internet. As a result, Chieko was inducted into the National Inventors Hall of Fame.

Travis Kalanick and Garrett Camp

Why did taxi companies not innovate? Why did they not take advantage of new technologies to improve services and expand their customer base? They had a good run until Travis Kalanick and Garrett Camp saw the crack in the wall. These guys saw the services that taxi companies failed to provide and seized the opportunity to create Uber—the taxi of the future.

Brian Chesky, Joe Gebbia and Nathan Blecharczyk

Hotels used to be an indispensable part of the hospitality and lodging market. Not anymore. That reached an end when the unthinkable happened: Brian Chesky, Joe Gebbia and Nathan Blecharczyk saw a gap in the line of defense of the hotel industry and went straight through it. And just like that, Airbnb was born in 2008.

George Washington Carver

Lots of people saw, ate or used peanuts. But the American agricultural scientist, George Washington Carver, saw beyond the traditional use of peanut. Therefore, he developed about 325 different uses for peanuts, such as cooking oil and ink, to name a few.

The PayPal mafia

The PayPal mafia gave us a way to make online payments while the big banks were enjoying their past successes and profits and sitting on piles of cash.

Seth Godin

Seth Godin debunked fake marketing, redefined what effective marketing should look like, and published the books *Purple Cow, This is Marketing* and *Tribes* to lead the way to a better way of doing marketing—and teach lessons worth sharing with one's colleagues and friends.

Victor B. Lawrence

The distinguished professor, researcher and scientist, Victor Lawrence, made worldwide communications networks possible and changed the world for the better.

He helped the Internet go global. His inventions and work improved signal transmission and made high-speed connections available across the globe. He also made it possible for us to watch TV on our smartphones by improving data encoding and audio and digital-video coding.

Good seeing skills

The above examples illustrate how the protagonists observed and saw gaps in the market many companies and people overlooked. The people in these examples took on the challenges, thought about solutions and brought changes and innovation.

These folks filled the gaps with brand-new messages or better products that resonate with most consumers. They even accomplished what most people thought was impossible. What should we learn from these changemakers?

While the inability to see becomes a huge impediment that prevents most professionals from breaking away from competition, it presents an invaluable opportunity for those with excellent seeing skills—those who can pay attention and listen carefully—to lead the way forward into the future.

The bottom line is that having seeing skills and focusing your attention matter. As Kevin Kelly, author of *The Inevitable* and founding executive editor of *Wired* magazine, said, "Since it is the last scarcity, wherever attention flows, money will follow." You get the point, don't you?

Imagine if you could identify and help solve the problems that keep your boss awake at night, or if you could create a product most did not even know they needed. Yes, it takes gut, boldness and audacity. But how different would your life be?

What can underdogs and undervalued employees do?

Career Move #9 – Develop sharp seeing skills and pay close attention.

What good is it to see and do what everybody sees and does? That automatically puts you in the kingdom of the average. The competition is brutal at this level. You can't shine there. The secret is, as Seth Godin said, "You cannot be seen unless you learn to see." That is, invisible talents or underdogs who want to raise their profile ought to learn to see beyond the obvious. And the best way to do it is to have a system or follow conceptual frameworks. When you see clearly, you can start thinking about solutions. You can take action to make contributions worth talking about. As soon as your best work gets noticed, you will become more visible—and valuable.

Paying attention is an excellent way to identify issues and solutions. The more problems you help solve, the more employers need you and the further you will be from the competition in the job market. Isn't that what you want?

What it takes to develop excellent seeing skills

> Developing excellent seeing skills requires time, curiosity and focus. It requires a commitment to questioning even what you think you already know well. More importantly, it requires that you rise above your own biases to see better and more clearly. Why? Because our own brain stands in the way of our genius.

It also requires you to regulate and control your urge to be right and to be "normal." It requires you to resist the urge to be "connected" to social media and gadgets 100% of the time.

Above all, it means dealing with and conquering what's called FOMO: the Fear of Missing Out. It's about asking the right questions—even the hard ones. Questioning our own points of view and stepping away from our personal experiences and knowledge is the way to go.

Taking action

You should have a way, or a system, to explore work situations and ask yourself these questions:

- What opportunities does this situation bring?
- What don't I see or understand about recurring issues?
- What information am I missing?
- What keeps management awake at night?
- What are other people afraid of and why?
- What are the market trends?
- What is holding my company back?
- What's my company's edge?
- What is management not saying?
- What does my boss need in order to do his job more effectively?
- What should be improved or done differently?

Developing seeing skills is a commitment to be different; to see beyond your experience, knowledge and biases; and to put a dent in projects and in your company's story by bringing solutions your employer or the market didn't even know was needed.

Being able to see and think critically is important. But taking action—execution—is a different beast. We'll talk about it in the next chapter.

Reflection questions

- How do I disconnect myself from the tech world and for how long should I disconnect?
- What trends should I pay attention to?
- How do I screen the information I consume?
- What work assumptions do I need to investigate?
- In what ways am I thinking for myself?
- What limitations do I need to investigate?

CHAPTER 10

Leading Instead of Hiding

See, think, do.

- What products are you creating right now?
- What did you create in the past few months?
- What are your concrete and distinct realizations?
- What do you have to show for your years of experience?
- What do you keep in your professional portfolio, if you have one?

You cannot contribute if you don't know how to execute. You can't be a problem-solver if you fail to contribute. The art of contribution and the skills of execution walk hand in hand. In other words, a key differentiator among professionals is the willingness and ability to execute good ideas.

- Seth Godin says he doesn't think there is a shortage of good ideas and opportunities to carry them out. Instead, he says, "Nope, what's missing isn't the ideas. It's the will to execute them."
- To rise and stay above the competition, you ought to be more than an idea generator, creator and collector because, as Scott Adams argued, "The market rewards execution, not ideas."
- Peter Drucker took the idea of execution one step further by arguing, "Intelligence, imagination, and knowledge are essential resources, but only effectiveness converts them into results. By themselves, they only set limits to what can be attained."

- Creating plans and strategies are great. But failing to execute and produce tangible results is almost like calling yourself an "investor" when you never invest a penny in the market.

Examples of execution

Ben Carson

As a young pediatric neurosurgeon at the John Hopkins Hospital, Dr. Ben Carson, did his homework, put in the hours and achieved in 1987 what used to be impossible. He led a team that performed one of the most challenging neurosurgeries in the world: he separated conjoined twins. In doing so, he put John Hopkins Hospital on the map and became a pioneer in his field.

Jonathan Edward Favreau

Not many people know of the speechwriter, Favreau, the architect of Obama's inaugural speech. No one can downplay his contribution to the Obama brand.

Jon Favreau started as Senator Obama's speechwriter. He helped the senator send clear messages that captured the attention of his constituency and the American people. Later on, Favreau helped the presidential candidate shape a narrative that resonated with the majority of the American people.

After Obama won the 2008 election, Jon Favreau got promoted and joined the White House as Director of Speechwriting. President Obama has referred to Favreau as his "mind reader." That said, we can safely say Favreau has delivered on the promise to make the former senator look and sound great. This is an example of execution.

Senator Orrin Hatch

Senators have the same title and work in the same chamber, but they are not equally effective and productive. According to the Library of Congress, Senator Orrin Hatch, although unknown to most Americans as I write this, is the most prolific lawmaker on Capitol Hill. He has a total of 742 laws under his belt. To be specific, Senator Orrin Hatch sponsored and co-sponsored 742 bills. Thus, when it comes to talking about the art of execution or getting things done in Congress, Orrin Hatch can raise his hand without hesitation.

What can underdogs and undervalued employees do?

Career Move #10 – Execute your promises and get the right things done.

> You don't need to be Albert Einstein to know getting the wrong things done makes you look busy, but it is risky. It's a terrible mistake. A waste of time. And it leads nowhere.

In fact, spending time and energy on the wrong things is like your car getting stuck in the mud with no forward traction and you pressing the gas pedal until your car runs out of gas.

Bill Belichick is no stranger to the art of execution. He consistently reminds his players to be consistent, pay attention to details and execute. And "do your job" became Bill Belichick's mantra, the statement he became known for.
We both know what the man achieves and represents in the National Football League.

What the art of execution looks like in a workday

The main focus of your professional career *is to be effective and useful*. To transform your ability and knowledge into concrete results. To get the right things done.

Peter Drucker pointed out that if we can't increase a resource's supply, we need to increase its yield. He added, "And effectiveness is the one tool to make the resources of ability and knowledge yield more and better results." Making execution the main focus of your career is a commitment to...

- Keep your promises.

- Work well with others to get the work done.
- Take concrete actions that drive change in your department without being asked to.
- Take initiatives and risks that others won't take without being asked to.
- Create products that make your boss look great.
- Find new information or data your company desperately needs.
- Solve interesting problems —especially those that keep management awake at night.
- Go beyond your job description and contribute without asking for permission.
- Build a portfolio worth talking about.

In other words, you should eat and breathe effectiveness, doing work your boss and your company need, rather than doing what you desire. Doing so consistently will increase your value in the job market and turn you into a linchpin most leaders want on their team.

Stop at nothing

Don't let people's degrees or diplomas fool you. Many might say without those letters after your name, you don't have what it takes. When they doubt you, you have two options: Get scared, hide and do nothing, or use their critiques to fuel your motivation and desire to execute your promises.

> Either way, you will be criticized for doing nothing or your work will be criticized. It's better to have work that people can talk about.

Keep in mind, as Peter Drucker argued, "To be reasonably effective, it is not enough for the individual to be intelligent, to work hard, or to be knowledgeable. Effectiveness is something separate, something different. But to be effective also does not require special gifts, special aptitude, or special training."

Seth Godin points out that you will face two options at the end of the day: "to be invisible, anonymous, uncriticized, and safe, or to take a chance at greatness, uniqueness, and the Cow." By "the Cow," he means remarkable work.

Below are examples of things you can execute:

- The implementation of strategies and plans
- Root-cause analysis and possible interventions
- Gap analysis and possible interventions
- Data collection, analysis and potential interventions
- Market research, trend analysis and possible actions
- Presentations on key issues
- Standard operating procedures
- Customer service inadequacies and solutions

A key factor in executing your promises is to build and use friendly and productive relationships with key players and decision-makers so you can navigate workplace red tape and office politics to move your ideas forward. Otherwise, it will be almost impossible to accomplish anything, especially in a hostile and toxic work environment.

For more on this, let's go to the next chapter.

Reflection questions

- What is my team missing?
- What deficiency do I notice and where?
- What concrete products can I create?
- What products can I improve?

Creating winning career systems

CHAPTER 11

Invisible Career Traps and Killers

The most dangerous career destroyers are hidden, unwritten and unspoken rules. And failing to keep them in mind will hold you back. It doesn't matter that you have talent and expertise. Acting in accordance with these rules is even more critical for underdogs and undervalued talents. Really?

> All institutions have established political systems in which most staff compete to maintain control, influence and power, even when they claim to be excellent team players.

For example, the first unspoken rule is that you work for your supervisor, not for a company. Companies are ideas in our heads. Thus, your success, for the major part, depends on your ability to support and work well with your boss—regardless of his qualifications and temperament. Don't believe me? Ask your company for a good recommendation and see what happens.

The roadblock

Employees cannot execute and contribute to their organization's mission if they are unable to navigate invisible and unspoken rules: workplace conflicts, problems and drama. Working well with others represents a *sine qua non* condition for talents who want to be useful.

Peter Drucker explained that a worker who produces knowledge, ideas or information does not create something that is effective by itself. "By themselves, these 'products' are useless," he says.

You and your best ideas, in isolation or outside of a system, are useless at best. You can't drive changes, innovation and transformation by yourself. You need colleagues and supervisors to use your ideas, work and products. Otherwise, your labor is in vain.

An isolated and individualistic employee who attempts to make a significant impact alone is like a pilot who refuses to collaborate with crew members, control towers and FAA authorities, while still hoping to fly the plane, reach the destination and land safely.

That pilot may be well trained, experienced and knowledgeable, but his chance of success is close to zero. Many employees indeed face tremendous challenges in the job market. Some are the target of workplace jokes, lies and manipulation.

What's worse, most are underpaid, misunderstood and undervalued. However, they should never let their situations cause them to hurt their reputation and lose key recommendations and relationships. Failing to manage office politics and losing one's composure at the workplace is playing right into the hands of one's detractors—and competitors.

Kawhi Leonard

Famous pro basketball player, Kawhi Leonard, led Canada's Toronto Raptors to their first NBA championship in 2019. But do you know what his detractors had said about him? Many underestimated his ability and said, "He's not a leader. He doesn't have what it takes. He is not as good as Lebron James." The media got all over him, making comparisons to other players and pressing his buttons. But Kawhi remained calm and focused.

Sportswriter, Zito Madu, of the blogging network, *SB Nation,* wrote this: "While Leonard's laconic interviews and stoic attitude make him an easy target for jokes, that unflappable demeanor is his most powerful weapon. It has transformed the Raptors, once known as perennial choke artists, into a team that never gets flustered." Kawhi's demeanor shows he understands and masters the game of NBA politics, media manipulation and personal power. This leads us to the main point of this chapter.

What can underdogs and undervalued employees do?

Career Move #11 – Leverage your inner power—your attitude.

Managing your attitude and developing sharp emotional-intelligence skills are critical to your success. It's tied to how you understand and deal with power dynamics, hierarchy and status—the unspoken rules—in organizations and society in general.

The way you act and react to people's actions and decisions determines whether you are in control of your life and professional career.

Frankly, these types of skills determine how high you'll get on the success ladder. They help avoid self-inflicting harm and disastrous situations.

For example, attitude and emotional intelligence made Nelson Mandela president of South Africa, immortalized Martin Luther King Jr., and transformed Kawhi Leonard into a hero in the NBA.

The secret is, as Scott Adams said, "If you could control your attitude directly, as opposed to letting the environment dictate how you feel on any given day, it would be like a minor superpower."

Then he added, "It turns out you have that superpower." And guess what? This power has stood the test of time, and nobody can take it away from you.

Helpful connections

To build helpful connections and relationships, a positive attitude is necessary. And connections are indispensable for success. Let me explain:

- As famous consultant, speaker and author, Peter Block, explained, "We must establish a personal connection with each other. Connection before content. Without relatedness, no work can occur."
- Building connections requires that we invest time and energy, intentionally connecting with people on a personal level. That is, getting to know coworkers as people with interests, weaknesses and strengths.
- Building connections also means going beyond using colleagues to get what one needs. It's rather a genuine interest in other individuals—in their interests and passion. Why is that?

People enjoy collaborating and conducting business with folks they know, like and trust. The more connected we are, the easier it is for our career in terms of finding opportunities and making contributions— that is, to flourish.

But it's hard to build a strong, wide network or strong social capital with a stinking, noxious and unpleasant attitude. Most of the time, a positive attitude trumps skills, knowledge and experience.

It's the kind of wind energy that can propel your career boat forward in the right direction. A positive attitude helps build, influence and find the common ground that leads to opportunities.

As Robert B. Cialdini, psychology professor and author of *Influence: The Psychology of Persuasion,* explained, "Attractiveness, similarity, compliments, contact and cooperation can make a person more influential."

What cultivating a positive attitude means

> Cultivating a positive attitude means to stay in control in all situations. To see the good in everyone or every situation. To spread a good vibe even under pressure. And to stay on the right side of people—especially of influencers, leaders and decision-makers.

Here are a few action steps that can reinforce your positive outlook and make you more attractive as a professional:

- Respect people's status, hierarchy and power.
- Avoid being defensive and self-righteous.
- Use empathy—put yourself in others' shoes.
- Avoid competing and comparing yourself with others.
- Assume responsibility for your own actions.
- Master office politics and unspoken rules.
- Avoid complaining and being vocal about other people.
- Welcome and use feedback to your advantage.
- Avoid being critical and judgmental towards others.
- Celebrate and compliment others often.
- Show genuine interest in your colleagues and supervisor.
- Make people feel comfortable around you.
- Put your team and company first in everything.

Workplace foolishness

Finally, avoid using criticism against your fellow workers—or anyone else. Criticizing your colleagues is a fatal mistake that will earn you lots of enemies—and it will come back to bite you.

Let me be the first to say that this is hard to follow, especially when you are trying hard to build connections and get along with colleagues. The best you can do is to resist the temptation diplomatically.

The danger is, as the famous author and lecturer Dale Carnegie said, "Criticism is futile because it puts a person on the defensive and usually makes him strive to justify himself. Criticism is dangerous, because it wounds a person's precious pride, hurts his sense of importance, and arouses resentment....Any fool can criticize, condemn, and complain—and most fools do. But it takes character and self-control to be understanding and forgiving."

The question is this: Do you want to be a fool or an understanding and forgiving person? The decision is yours to make.

Harnessing your attitude is even more effective when coupled with super skills—or the ability to adjust and change fast. We'll cover this in the next chapter.

Reflection questions

- Do I know what triggers me?
- How sharp is my emotional intelligence?
- What do I do to tame my ego?
- What activities can help me improve my EQ?

CHAPTER 12

Creating the Future

The world—and the job market—is changing without asking our permission. Innovation does not plan to wait on us. What's worse, things took an unexpected turn with the COVID-19 pandemic. For many companies and their employees, regardless of their preferences, teleworking suddenly became the norm.

The next big thing got here before one knew it. As Kevin Kelly explained, "We are morphing so fast that our ability to invent new things outpaces the rate we can civilize them."

You can already guess what this trend means for professionals who want to remain relevant, useful and competitive: more technology and more artificial intelligence (AI) in the workplace. Even worse, within just a few months, COVID-19 took this trend to the next level.

In his book, *The Inevitable*, Kevin Kelly shared this staggering observation: "Uber, the world's largest taxi company, owns no vehicles. Facebook, the world's most popular media owner, creates no content. Alibaba, the most valuable retailer, has no inventory. And Airbnb, the world's largest accommodation provider, owns no real estate. Something interesting is happening."

We live in a world where most new companies rely heavily on technology. To remain competitive and in business, most old companies have tried to reinvent themselves by investing more and more in technology and AI. The consequences?

Workers who are unable or unwilling to reinvent themselves become more dispensable than ever before. Now, with COVID-19, U.S. workers have no choice but to embrace

Creating winning career systems

technology. This chapter was written before COVID-19, but I've updated it to share some insights that are relevant to life in a post-COVID-19 world. Below is the data and information I shared before COVID-19.

Drones in the job market

> It's too bad that many professionals still think their employers will protect their jobs or shield their careers from the AI effect. I hope you are not one of them.

The use of Unmanned Aerial Vehicles (UAVs), commonly called drones, is increasing rapidly. The use of drones had a growth rate of 19% in 5 years, from 2015 to 2020, according to *Business Insider*. Based on the current trend, this technology is on track to replace thousands of pilots, soldiers and delivery drivers. How so?

Divya Joshi, a writer at *Business Insider*, reported: "Whether drones are controlled by a remote or accessed via a smartphone app, they possess the capability of reaching the most remote areas with little to no manpower needed and require the least amount of effort, time, and energy. This is one of the biggest reasons why they are being adopted worldwide, especially by these four sectors: Military, Commercial, Personal, and Future Technology."

Elon Musk's prediction

Elon Musk, founder and CEO of Tesla and SpaceX, took this trend 100 steps further by making a bold prediction. "Drone warfare is where the future will be. It's not that I want the future to be—it's just, this is what the future will be," he said.

He also said that the U.S. F-35 fighter jet should have a competitor, and wrote, "The competitor should be a drone fighter plane that's remote-controlled by a human, but with its maneuvers augmented by autonomy. The F-35 would have no chance against it."

Elon Musk might be onto something. Yes, indeed—as always. And don't bet against him. You will lose. How do I know? General Salami of Iran was killed in January 2020 by a drone strike, not by a living and breathing soldier on the ground.

This increase in drone usage is innovation at its best, but it's bad news for delivery drivers, jet fighter pilots, soldiers and workers who are currently doing jobs UAVs can do faster, better and at a lower cost.

Education left the classroom

The demand for online education is increasing rapidly, and college and university professors have no choice but to embrace this new reality.

For example, Jordan Friedman, a contributor of *U.S. News*, wrote in January 2018 that "Based on federal data from more than 4,700 colleges and universities, more than 6.3 million students in the U.S.—most of whom were undergraduates—took at least one online course in fall 2016, a 5.6 percent increase from the previous year. This is the 14th consecutive year that Babson has reported growth in online enrollment."
The question is this: What will happen to traditional professors who are not willing or cannot facilitate online learning? Sooner or later they will have to adjust—or throw in the towel.

Robots in the marketplace

According to the *U.S. Census Bureau News* published in February 2020, sales at traditional stores declined in the past year while E-commerce's retail sales increased to 11% from 6%. But there's more:

- Brick-and-mortar stores give jobs to millions of people compared to their online competitors that operate with fewer employees. With this growing trend in sales, many traditional stores will shut down and millions of traditional workers will go unemployed unless they learn new skills and find other opportunities in the job market.

- According to Sapna Maheshwari of *The NY Times*, the U.S. economy lost about 6,000 traditional stores in 2018 alone. And things are not getting better for traditional retailers. Where does that leave their employees?

- The Bureau of Labor Statistics predicts a decrease of 2% in retail sales jobs from 2018 to 2028. And its website forecasts that "Competition from online sales will lead to employment decline in brick-and-mortar retail stores." Where will that leave traditional workers?

Many believe that more-educated workers and high-paying jobs are safe from the AI and tech effect. Well, not so fast. Advanced technologies keep breaking new limits and can perform complex tasks as well.

For example, the United States Government Accountability Office, in its report to Congress on workforce automation that was titled "Better Data Needed to Assess and Plan for Effects of Advanced Technologies on Jobs," shared a list of occupations (environmental engineering technicians, broadcast technicians, municipal firefighters, electrical power-line installers and repairers, painters and transportation equipment) that already use AI as a daily tool.

The title of the report says it all: There's not enough data to determine the impact of advanced technology in the job market. Therefore, many professionals might get blindsided and caught unprepared when AI makes their jobs obsolete in a blink of an eye.

Post-COVID-19 observations

As I finalized this chapter during the COVID-19 crisis, it's worth adding some further observations.

K-12 schools, colleges and universities took their classes online, and now most teachers and professors face a new reality: teaching in an environment most of them do not know well or do not control.

Nor do they have the appropriate training to quickly adapt face-to-face instruction to distance learning.

Not only learning institutions were affected. Lots of companies turned to telework. So, many employees found themselves in a telework environment and in situations that look like unknown territory.

As a result, the career move below that I wrote before the pandemic became even more critical in a post-COVID-19 world, especially for underdogs who want to be relevant in the job market.

What can underdogs and undervalued employees do after COVID-19?

Career Move #12 – Develop your ability to adjust and change fast—to reinvent yourself.

We can do work that protects the status quo by fighting changes and innovation, and we can hide in our comfort zone, hoping retirement will arrive before a major market shift happens. But this is a risky move. As a matter of fact, COVID-19 already changed the game.

> Our skills and knowledge might become obsolete and get replaced by AI before we know it. Thus, a better alternative is to become lifelong learners who adjust, embrace change, lead the way—and help create the future. This is indispensable in this new world.

That said, adaptability skills (AQ) have become as important as knowledge and emotional intelligence (EQ), and those who adjust fast enough will remain relevant and have a better chance of surviving the COVID-19 crisis, including dodging the AI bullet.

Where to start...

The point is, as Alvin Toffler said,

"To survive, to avert what we have termed future shock, the individual must become infinitely more adaptable and capable than ever before. We must search out totally new ways to anchor ourselves, for all the old roots – religion, nation, community, family, or profession – are now shaking under the hurricane impact of the accelerative thrust. It is no longer resources that limit decisions, it is the decision that makes the resources."

- Therefore, avoid betting on jobs that pay you to fight change or that AI will eradicate in the next five years. They are not promising, rewarding and future-oriented. And such jobs eventually will lead to loss, pain and career disaster.
- Instead, embracing change and learning new skills is the best way forward into the next decade and generation. Changing with the job market is a key strategy in the post-COVID-19 job market.
- Having a PD system in place is a good way to track your trends and evolution in your field. It helps you stay informed, learn new skills, and make systematic career moves to get and stay ahead of the curve.

To that effect, one must make AI an ally, not the enemy. As Kevin Kelly explained, "This is not a race against the machines.

If we race against them, we lose. This is a race with the machines. You'll be paid in the future based on how well you work with robots. Ninety percent of your coworkers will be unseen machines."

Turning AI into your ally in this post-COVID-19 world is critical to your success. But how do you do that?

By doing this:

- Do work that AI cannot perform well. Leverage your soft and people skills.
- Learn to work and collaborate with AI (tools and software).
- Use AI to increase your performance and concentration.
- Leverage and use AI (tools and software) to improve your skills and your work—and your craft.

Being able to adjust, change and learn fast is what I call having super skills– skills that might be necessary for your survival in a post-COVID-19 job search and competitive marketplace.

Sharpening these skills is a commitment to creating the future you desire instead of staying stuck in the past. It's a choice to become a lifelong learner who can use new technology or AI to reinvent himself or herself over and over again, as many times as necessary.

Reflection questions

- Am I always aware of the latest development in my field?
- How sharp are my soft skills and people skills?
- How well do I deal with change?
- Considering my field of work, am I ahead or behind the curve?
- What decision can I take now to better prepare myself for a post-COVID-19 job market?

CONCLUSION

Now what?

As we've discussed, the job market is competitive, unpredictable and continuously changing. So, it's hard to rely on job security and your company's performance and market trends when you are an underdog or undervalued talent.

We've also discussed that you can rely on work security, instead of job security, when you offer world-class services and solutions the world needs. Because the market never stops searching for "better." This also means you don't have to remain an underdog forever.

It's obvious that building a rewarding career while making a difference in the world requires intense emotional labor. But what other choice do underdogs like us have?

We could remain stuck in average work, hide in our comfort zone, and spend our time and energy on jobs we don't like, doing things we don't even care about. But we cannot afford to make this mistake. It's not worth it.

A better choice is to offer the world your best work and claim your spot among the leading voices in your field. This means to do the following:

- Show up every day with the purpose to serve.
- Do things that keep customers happy and your boss proud.
- Make decisions that make your employers profitable.
- Take actions that keep clients coming back for more.

Expertise coupled with a portfolio worth showing and talking about will make you not a professional underdog, but a visible talent that most employers and supervisors wish they had on their team.

But to build this kind of career requires a systematic view and approach of our career development. It requires systems to help you override lack of willpower and procrastination to build a fulfilling career and make a difference in the world—and in your world.

That's it for me. Now, what will you do with this information?

I really hope these pages help you prepare for your next career moves, whatever they may be, especially in a post-COVID-19 world. I cannot wait to meet you and hear from you.

One small favor: Would you gift this book to a friend—or an undervalued talent—who's looking for helpful professional insights and guidance? Thanks.

Further Reading

As you work on building career-development systems, consider reading and adding these books to your arsenal:

- *Talking to Strangers: What We Should Know about the People We Don't Know* by Malcolm Gladwell
- *This Is Marketing: You Can't Be Seen Until You Learn to See* by Seth Godin
- *Purple Cow: Transform Your Business by Being Remarkable* by Seth Godin
- *The Inevitable: Understanding the 12 Technological Forces That Will Shape Our Future* by Kevin Kelly
- *How to Fail at Almost Everything and Still Win Big: Kind of the Story of My Life* by Scott Adams
- *Mastery* by Robert Greene
- *Deep Work: Rules for Focused Success in a Distracted World* by Cal Newport
- *My Philosophy For Successful Living* by Jim Rohn
- *The Effective Executive: The Definitive Guide to Getting the Right Things Done* by Peter F. Drucker
- *The Infinite Game* by Simon Sinek
- *Choose Yourself! Be Happy, Make Millions, Live the Dream* by James Altucher
- *The Essential Deming: Leadership Principles from the Father of Quality* by W. Edwards Deming
- *Zero to One: Notes on Startups, or How to Build the Future* by Peter Thiel and Blake Masters
- *Ego Is the Enemy* by Ryan Holiday

- *Turning Pro: Tap Your Inner Power and Create Your Life's Work* by Steven Pressfield and Shawn Coyne
- *The War of Art: Break Through the Blocks and Win Your Inner Creative Battles* by Steven Pressfield and Shawn Coyne
- *Mindset: The New Psychology of Success* by Carol S. Dweck
- *How to Win Friends & Influence People* by Dale Carnegie
- *You've Got To Be Hungry: The Greatness Within to Win* by Les Brown and Ona Brown
- *Soar! Build Your Vision from the Ground Up* by T. D. Jakes
- *Instinct: The Power to Unleash Your Inborn Drive* by T. D. Jakes
- *In Pursuit of Purpose: The Key to Personal Fulfillment* by Myles Munroe and Ben Kinchlow
- *Becoming* by Michelle Obama
- *Daring Greatly: How the Courage to Be Vulnerable Transforms the Way We Live, Love, Parent, and Lead* by Brené Brown
- *21 Lessons for the 21st Century* by Yuval Noah Harari
- *The Black Swan: Second Edition: The Impact of the Highly Improbable* by Nassim Nicholas Taleb
- *The 15 Invaluable Laws of Growth: Live Them and Reach Your Potential* by John Maxwell
- *Influence: The Psychology of Persuasion* by Robert B. Cialdini

Interesting and Relevant podcasts

Below is a list of podcasts I have found relevant to personal growth. Feel free to check them out.

- *The School of Greatness* with Lewis Howes
- *Impact Theory* with Tom Bilyeu
- *Revisionist History* with Malcolm Gladwell
- *The Prof G Show* with Scott Galloway
- *Super Soul Sunday* with Oprah Winfrey
- *TED Radio Hour* with Alison Stewart, Guy Raz and Manoush Zomorodi
- *Radiolab* with Jad Abumrad and Robert Krulwich
- *This American Life* with Ira Glass
- *It's Been a Minute* with Sam Sanders
- *Hidden Brain* with Shankar Vedantam

Acknowledgment

Few of the ideas in the chapters are my own. I've read and learned from a variety of sources and many giants and trailblazers in the marketplace. And I owe an intellectual debt of gratitude to my mom, Marie Rosette Edouard, and to Scott Adams, Maya Angelou, James Altucher, Les Brown, Peter Block, Brené Brown, Edwards Deming, Peter Drucker, Carol S. Dweck, Robert Green, Seth Godin, Malcolm Gladwell, Yuval Noah Harari, Ryan Holiday, TD Jakes, Kevin Kelly, Martin Luther King Jr., John Maxwell, Cal Newport, Steven Pressfield, Jim Rhon, Simon Sinek, Nassim Nicholas Taleb, Peter Thiel, Brian Tracy and Oprah Winfrey.

References

Adams, S. (2013). *How to Fail at Almost Everything and Still Win Big: Kind of the Story of My Life.* Penguin Publishing Group.

Altucher, J. (2015). *Choose Yourself!: Be Happy, Make Millions, live the Dream.* Brilliance Audio.

Block, P., & Markowitz, A. (2000). *The Flawless Consulting Fieldbook and Companion: A Guide to Understanding Your Expertise.* John Wiley & Sons.

Bureau of Labor Statistics. (2020). *Occupational Outlook Handbook, Retail Sales Workers.* U.S Bureau of Labor Statistics. https://www.bls.gov/ooh/sales/retailsalesworkers.htm

Carnegie, D. (2005). *How to Win Friends and Influence People.* Cornerstone Publishing.

Cialdini, R. B. (1993). *Influence: The Psychology of Persuasion (Rev. ed.).* New York: Quill/William Morrow.

Domo. (2020). *Data Never Sleeps 5.0.* Domo. https://www.domo.com/learn/data-never-sleeps-5?aid=ogsm072517_1&sf100871281=1

Drucker, P.F. (2017). *The Effective Executive: The Definitive Guide to Getting the Right Things Done.* HarperCollins.

Finkel, A. (2017, September 14). *The AC/DC current wars make a comeback.* Cosmos Magazine. https://cosmosmagazine.com/technology/tesla-vs-edison-the-ac-dc-current-wars-make-a-comeback

Friedman, J. (2018, January 11). *Study: More Students Are Enrolling in Online Courses.*

U.S.News. https://www.usnews.com/higher-education/online-education/articles/2018-01-11/study-more-students-are-enrolling-in-online-courses

GAO. (2019). *Workforce Automation: Better Data Needed to Assess and Plan for Effects of Advanced Technologies on Jobs*. US Government Accountability Office. https://www.gao.gov/assets/700/697366.pdf

Glaveski, S. (2019). *Where Companies Go Wrong with Learning and Development. Luettavissa:* https://hbr.org/2019/10/where-companies-go-wrong-with-learning-and-development *Luettu*, *6*, 2020.

Greene, R. (2012). *Mastery*. Penguin Books.

Hanbury, M. (2019, June 06). *Jony Ive's Apple exit has been a 'long time in the making' after he was only turning up to the office twice a week*. Business Insider. https://www.businessinsider.com/jony-ive-apple-exit-long-time-in-the-making-2019-6

Harari, Y. N. (2018). *21 Lessons for the 21st Century*. Random House.

Heath, C., & Heath, D. (2007). *Made to stick: Why Some Ideas Survive and Others Die*. Random House.

Houston, G. (2018, March 04). *Who Was Marie Callender?* MyRecipes. https://www.myrecipes.com/news/who-was-marie-callender

Joshi, D. (December 2019). *Drone technology uses and applications for commercial, industrial and military drones in 2021 and the future*. Business Insider. https://www.businessinsider.com/drone-technology-uses-applications

Kelly, K. (2017). *The Inevitable: Understanding the 12 Technological Forces That Will Shape Our Future*. Penguin Books.

King Jr, M. L. (1967). *What Is Your Life's Blueprint?* https://singjupost.com/what-is-your-lifes-blueprint-by-dr-martin-luther-king-jr-full-transcript/2/

Kisiel, R. (2003, June 16). *Iacocca: From '56 for '56' to company president.* Automotive News. https://www.autonews.com/article/20030616/SUB/306160757/iacocca-from-56-for-56-to-company-president

Lambert, L. (2020, March 24). *'This is cataclysmic': The coronavirus could obliterate 5 million to 6 million jobs in March alone.* Fortune. https://fortune.com/2020/03/24/coronavirus-unemployment-claims-layoffs-jobs-lost-us-march-2020/

Macias, A. (2020, February 28). *Elon Musk tells a room full of Air Force pilots: 'The fighter jet era has passed.'* CNBC. https://www.cnbc.com/2020/02/28/elon-musk-says-the-fighter-jet-era-has-passed.html

Madu, Z. (2019, June 8). *Kawhi Leonard is the perfect leader for the Raptors.* SBNATION. https://www.sbnation.com/2019/6/8/18657581/kawhi-leonard-raptors-warriors-nba-finals-leadership

Maheshwari, S. (2019, April 12). *U.S. Retail Stores' Planned Closings Already Exceed 2018 Total.* The New York Times. https://www.nytimes.com/2019/04/12/business/retail-store-closings.html

Masters, B., & Thiel, P. (2014). *Zero to One: Notes on Startups, or How to Build the Future.* Random House.

Maxwell, J. C. (2012). *The 15 Invaluable Laws of Growth: Live Them and Reach Your Potential.* Center Street.

McGrory, E. (2019, June 25). *Managing Personal Energy Gives Mom More Time.* The balance careers. https://www.thebalancecareers.com/managing-personal-energy-more-time-3544771

Munroe, M. (1992). *In Pursuit of Purpose: The Key to Personal Fulfillment*. Destiny Image Publishers.

Nair, R. (2015, May 27). *Internet & Mobile Phone Users Worldwide 2015: 50% Population Is On Internet [REPORT]*. Dazoinfo Briefs. https://dazeinfo.com/2015/05/27/internet-mobile-phone-users-worldwide-2000-2015-report/

National Inventors Hall of Fame. (2020). *The National Investors Hall of Fame Connects World-Changing Innovators with Today's Youth*. National Inventors Hall of Fame. https://www.invent.org/

Newport, C. (2016). *Deep Work: Rules for Focused Success in a Distracted World*. Hachette Audio UK.

Norman, J. (2018, August 28) Four in 10 U.S. *Workers Think They Are Underpaid*. Gallup. https://news.gallup.com/poll/241682/four-workers-think-underpaid.aspx

O'Connor, K. (2019, Jun 8). *How the Raptors Solved Steph Curry*. The Ringer. https://www.theringer.com/2019/6/8/18657848/toronto-raptors-steph-curry-defense

Puiu, T. (2020, February 11). *Your smartphone is millions of times more powerful than the Apollo 11 guidance computers*. ZME Science. https://www.zmescience.com/science/news-science/smartphone-power-compared-to-apollo-432/

Rob, A. (2016, February 02). *Toussaint Louverture: The First Successful Slave Revolt Leader*. Black History Month. https://www.blackhistorymonth.org.uk/article/section/history-of-slavery/4324/

Rohn, J. (2015). *Challenge to Succeed-A Philosophy for Successful Living Workbook*.

Roller, E., Stamm S. & National Journal. (2014, May 16). *Which Senator Has Passed the Most Laws?* The Atlantic.

https://www.theatlantic.com/politics/archive/2014/05/which-senator-has-passed-the-most-laws/455952/

Sinek, S. (2019). *The Infinite Game*. Penguin.

Toffler, A. (1984). *Future Shock*. Bantam.

Trading Economics. (2020). *United States Challenger Job Cuts*. Trading Economics. https://tradingeconomics.com/united-states/challenger-job-cuts

U.S. Census Bureau News. (2020). *Quarterly Retail E-Commerce Sales 1ˢᵗ Quarter 2020*. https://www.census.gov/retail/mrts/www/data/pdf/ec_current.pdf (Accessed: 10 June 2020).

Violita, E., & Pratiwy, D. (2019). Suffering in Chris Gardner's Autobiography: The Pursuit of Happyness. *Journal of Language, 1* (1), 11-24.

Index

Ally 78, 79
Artificial intelligence 73, 94
Attitude 69, 70, 71, 72
Authentic 11
Author 20, 38, 44, 57, 70, 72
Boss 6, 11, 23, 49, 50, 57, 59, 64, 67, 81
Career ii, x, xi, xii, xvi, xvii, 1, 3, 4, 5, 7, 9, 10, 11, 14, 15, 18, 20, 23, 27, 28, 29, 33, 35, 36, 37, 44, 45, 48, 49, 63, 67, 69, 70, 77, 78, 81, 82
Career development 24, 27, 29, 82
Champions xvi
Change xvi, 2, 3, 9, 45, 49, 64, 72, 77, 78, 79
Coach xiv, 19, 21, 33, 34, 42
Coaching ii, iii, xvi, 27, 28, 33, 34, 51
Colleagues 7, 11, 18, 26, 28, 50, 57, 68, 70, 71, 72
Company 4, 7, 10, 12, 15, 16, 18, 25, 36, 37, 51, 53, 59, 64, 67, 71, 73

Continuous Improvement 29, 95
Contribution 6, 47, 48, 61, 62
COVID-19 iii, x, xi, xvii, 2, 54, 73, 74, 76, 77, 78, 79, 82
Craft 10
Crisis iii, xi
Culture 16, 24, 26, 27, 51
Distraction 40, 54
Drone 74, 75
Employees iii, x, xii, xvii, 2, 3, 5, 7, 9, 12, 15, 16, 17, 23, 24, 25, 26, 27, 31, 37, 38, 42, 44, 49, 50, 58, 63, 67, 68, 69, 73, 75, 76, 77
Execution xvii, 59, 61, 62, 63
Expertise 3, 29, 41, 81,
Goals xvii, 29, 31
Growth x, xi, 26, 29, 44, 74, 75, 85, 94, 95
Hide 26, 64, 77, 81
Hiring manager 12, 13, 16, 41
Interesting problems 19, 64
Interview 12, 69
Jim Rhon 18, 86
Job xii, xv, xvii, 1, 2, 3, 4, 5, 8, 9, 10, 12, 13, 14,

16, 17, 25, 26, 27, 31, 32, 35, 38, 42, 47, 48, 49, 50, 58, 59, 64, 68, 73, 74, 76, 77, 78, 79, 81

Job market xvii, 2, 4, 8, 10, 17, 31, 32, 35, 38, 47, 49, 58, 64, 68, 73, 74, 76, 77, 78, 79, 81

Kevin Kelly 57, 73, 78, 83, 86

Lead 6, 10, 15, 16, 23, 29, 40, 44, 45, 54, 55, 56, 57, 76, 77, 78, 84, 94, 95

Les Brown 6, 84, 86

Linchpin xvi, 3, 18, 33, 37, 44, 50, 64

Martin Luther King Jr. 69, 86

Master 10, 21, 34, 36, 38, 71

Mastery xvii, 24, 34, 35, 37, 38, 39, 40, 83

Mission 10, 18, 50, 67

Myles Munroe 5, 84

Myth xvii

Noise 53, 55

Opportunity 10, 12, 13, 23, 37, 49, 53, 54, 56, 57

Oprah Winfrey 5, 15, 19, 85, 86

Pay attention 40, 57, 60, 63

PD systems 34

Peter Block 70, 86

Peter Drucker 6, 44, 47, 48, 61, 63, 64, 68, 86

Peter Thiel 44, 83, 86

Portfolio 12, 45, 64, 81

Professionals xi, xvi, xvii, 3, 7, 11, 20, 30, 33, 38, 41, 42, 43, 44, 47, 53, 57, 61, 73, 74 76, 94

Projects 20, 45, 47, 59

Remarkable work xii, 5, 16, 17, 18, 65

Robert Green 86

Scott Adams 6, 19, 21, 31, 32, 61, 69, 83, 86

Seeing skills 57, 58, 59

Sense of purpose 5, 6

Seth Godin 1, 5, 9, 10, 11, 37, 38, 56, 58, 61, 65, 83, 86

Simon Sinek 5, 83, 86

Solutions xvii, 45, 47, 51, 57, 58, 59, 65, 81

Solve problems 13

Speaker 1, 5, 6, 18, 19, 36, 38, 70, 94

Stress x

Success xi, xvii, 9, 15, 16, 37, 68, 69, 83, 84, 90

Supervisor 71

Systems xv, xvii, 26, 27, 29, 30, 31, 32, 34, 67, 82, 94, 95

TD Jakes 35, 36, 86

Technology 1, 13, 43, 54, 73, 74, 76, 79, 88

The future 49, 73, 74, 78, 79, 83

Time ii, xvii, 11, 15, 16, 18, 19, 21, 25, 26, 32,

33, 35, 36, 38, 40, 43, 50, 55, 63, 70, 81, 88
Training xvii, 21, 23, 24, 25, 26, 27, 28, 77
Undervalued employees iii, xii, 5, 12, 17, 27, 31, 38, 44, 49, 58, 63, 69, 77
Winning xv, 45
Winning systems xv
Work x, xii, xv, 1, 3, 4, 5, 6, 7, 8, 9, 10, 11, 12, 13, 14, 17, 18, 19, 20, 25, 31, 33, 37, 38, 40, 41, 42, 45, 48, 50, 51, 57, 58, 59, 60, 62, 64, 65, 67, 69, 70, 77, 79, 81, 83
Work experience 40, 41, 42, 45
Work with a sense of purpose 5, 6
Workplace x, xi, xvi, 11, 65, 67, 68, 71, 73

About the Author

Coach Teddy Edouard is a lifelong learner, public speaker, writer, blogger and vlogger. He is the founder of Coaching for Better Learning LLC, where he helps people and institutions build systems that lead to lasting improvement, growth and success.

He also teaches professionals how to protect their careers and use artificial intelligence (AI) as a career improvement ally. You can say "hello" to him on Twitter (TeddyISD) and LinkedIn.

About Coaching for Better Learning LLC

CBL helps build Continuous Improvement (CI) systems that lead to stress-free improvement, growth and sustainable success.

We offer reliable client-centered coaching services to help you face your challenges with more confidence and less anxiety. Visit us at https://coachingforbetterlearning.com/.

COACHING
FOR
BETTER
LEARNING

Made in the USA
Middletown, DE
02 July 2021